Learn the basics of brush lettering, happy mail, envelope art, and creative lettering projects YOU can do!

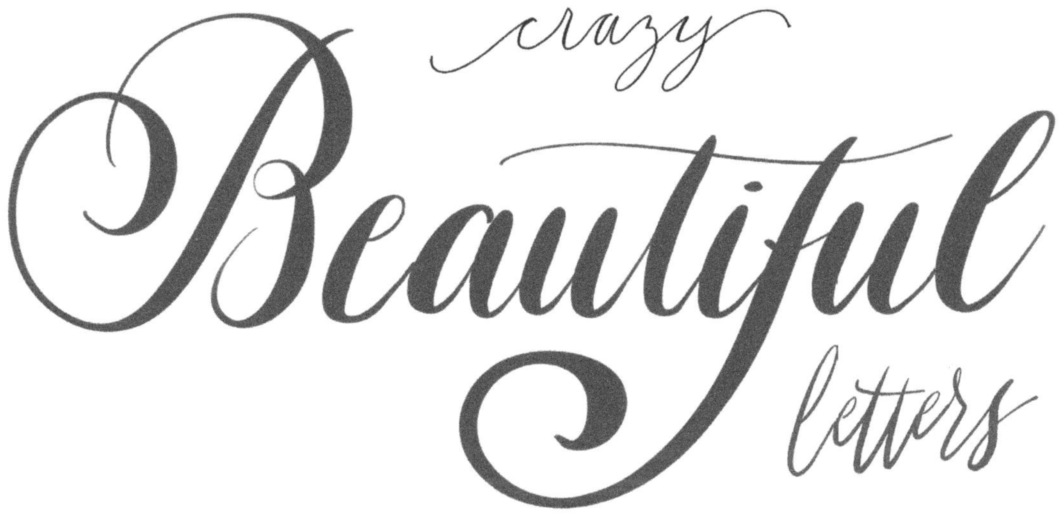

BY JUDITH GRAVES

Photography by Linda Goymer

Crazy Beautiful Letters: Learn the basics of brush lettering, happy mail, envelope art, and creative lettering projects YOU can do!

Illustrations by Judith Graves

Photography by Linda Goymer

(Except those on pages 6-7 by Judith Graves)

Sassy Lassie Designs
Cold Lake, Alberta. Canada.
https://sassylassiedesigns.ca

ISBN-13: 978-1-9995341-0-3 (Book)
ISBN-13: 978-1-9995341-1-0 (E-book)

Printed in the USA.

ALL THE THINGS

THE INTRODUCTION

THE GOODIES

THE SKILLS

THE LETTERFORMS

THE DETAILS

THE PROJECTS

THE HAPPY MAIL

THE TEMPLATES

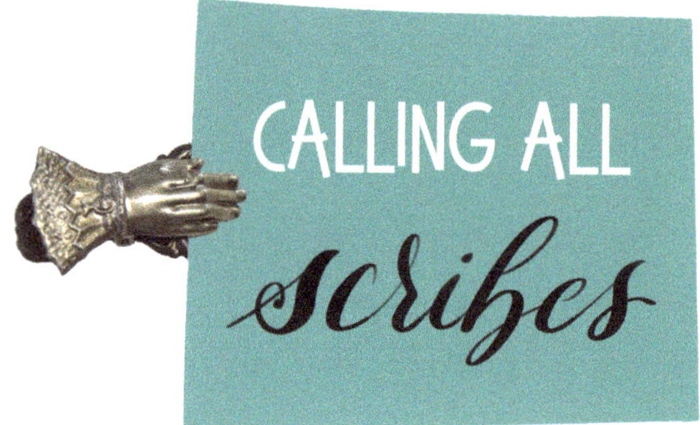

LET'S GET THIS OUT THERE,

right from the get go. I'm a genre fiction writer, writing primarily horror and thriller stories for young adults, but I write a bit of everything, for readers of all ages.

This is my first non-fiction effort. It is five galaxies and three parallel universes away from my writing comfort zone of blood, guts, and heartbreak. Chances are, if you're reading this book, or even skimming through the first few pages to see if it's worthy, you're in the same head space I occupied a few years ago. You want to challenge yourself, to take a small risk that might have long term personal growth and satisfaction payoff, and yet ... you hesitate. You have one foot firmly planted in routine and the familiar, and the other hovering over the glorious precipice known as, "I want to give this lettering and art thing a shot, but what if I suck?".

Congratulations! Self-doubt is part of the creative process. We've all been there. In fact, self-doubting-Judith (or Kate, or James, or insert-your-name-here) never really goes away. As Henri Matisse said, "Creativity takes courage." He sure wasn't kidding.

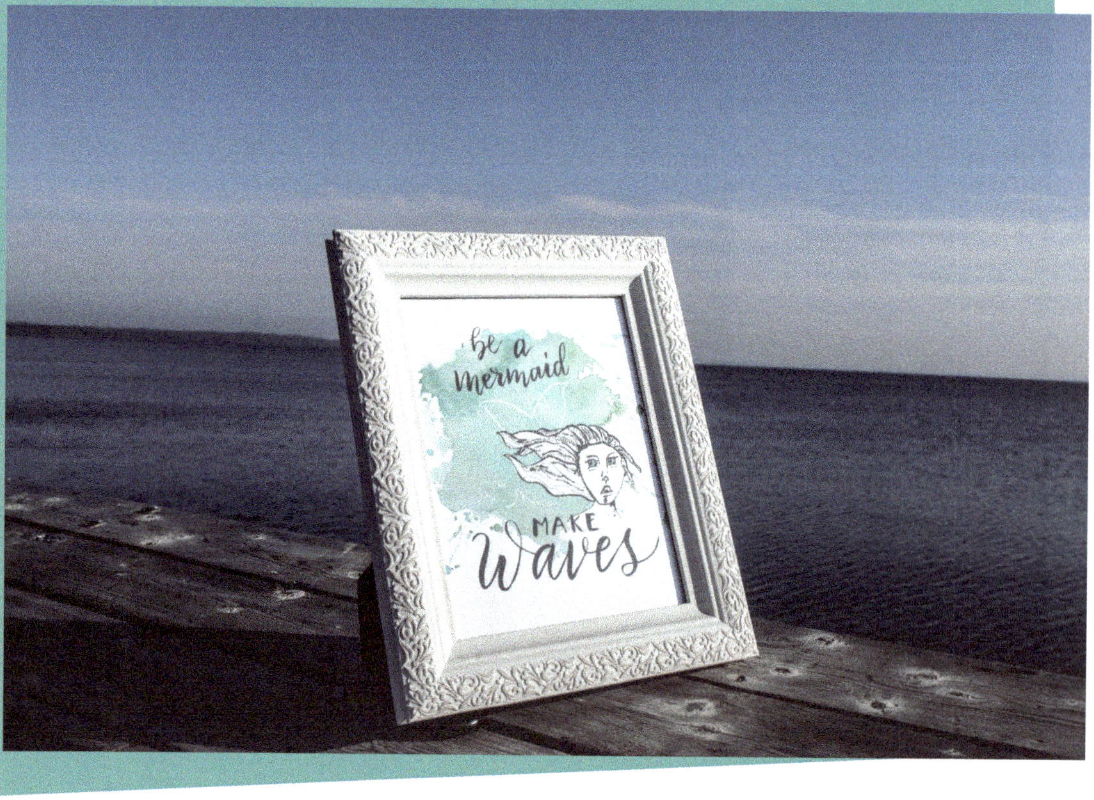

The trick is to take that oh-so-scary first step anyway. While I was able to dive into fiction writing, I kept my interest in graphic design, watercolour, lettering and typography on the fringe. With fiction I knew I could edit, revise, tweak, change, kill-off characters, and resurrect them. Writing is one big do-over until you get it right.

But art? There are no do-overs with art, right? Wrong. This is the pencil drafting and thumbnail sketch phase of layout and design where you're free to test, and try, and fail, and try again. It's like revisions in writing, only you doodle. It's fun, my friends. Not scary at all.

But art isn't something you can learn, you just have to have those skills in the womb. Right? Wrong again. Big time.

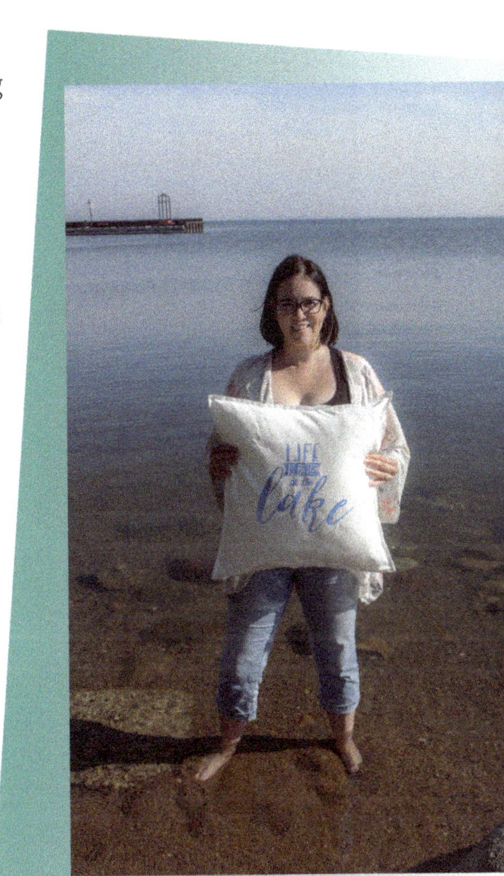

Drawing, painting, and lettering are skills you develop every time you give yourself permission to create. I'm not saying there aren't people who are more instinctively artistic than others. Of course there are. Just as there are people with more athletic ability or those who can do math. Any kind of math. Those people are freaking brilliant. But I am suggesting that with time, effort, and a willingness to work through the foundations, you can accomplish all kinds of artsy fartsy things. Like the skills, techniques, and projects in this book. You'll be a scribe in no time.

But what if your letterforms are wonky at first? Mine certainly were, and are, whenever I'm trying out a new style or script. Or if your lines are shaky? Or you used too much water and your watercolour paper warped? These are all common issues. Rites of passage, so to speak. If you're making mistakes, you're learning. If you're learning, you're building skill. If you've built skill, you can apply those skills to more advanced projects and keep learning. And so on, and so on.

It's time to let go of the need to be instantly good at something. Embrace the wonky. The crazy weird flower you just painted that doesn't look anything like your reference photo. It's all beautiful, because it's you, going for it. The more you art, the better you artist.

Alright, enough with the pep talk.

LET'S GO MAKE SOME CRAZY BEAUTIFUL LETTERS TOGETHER.

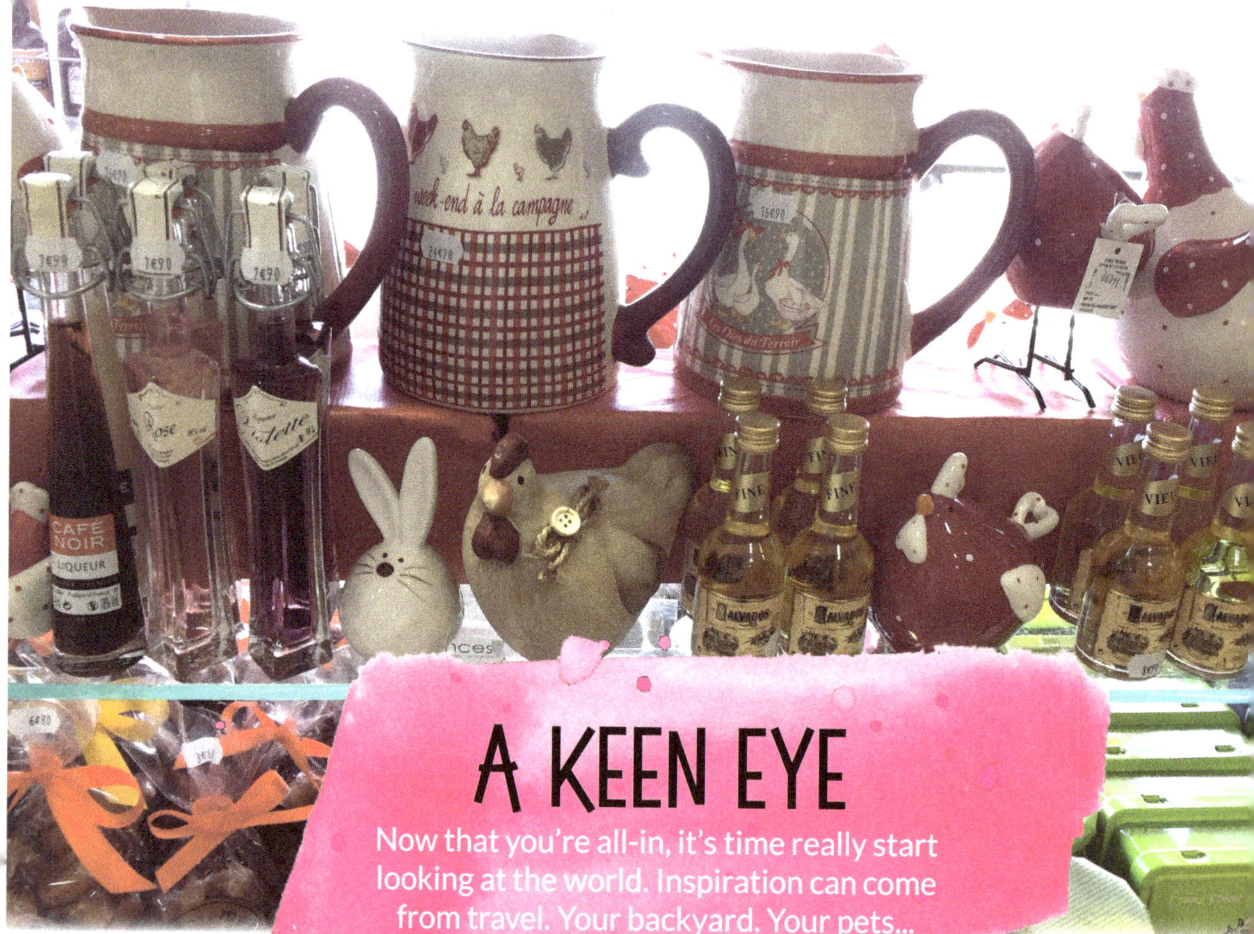

A KEEN EYE

Now that you're all-in, it's time really start looking at the world. Inspiration can come from travel. Your backyard. Your pets...

My husband and I love to travel. On our adventures, I take typical touristy pictures, but I also snap photos of signage, window displays, doors, textures, patterns, and anything else that catches my eye. I may be attracted to letterforms, layout, or a vivid palette of colours I want to document for use in projects when we're back at home.

Every place is unique. From window displays in a medieval village, to a flamboyant free-book exchange in New Orleans, each location has its own vibe and energy that is clearly visible with how they choose to letter their words.

But you don't have to hop on a plane to start developing your keen artist's eye. There's beauty all around us. This is your homework: start documenting the things you love. Zoom in on the small details, or pan out for the bigger picture.

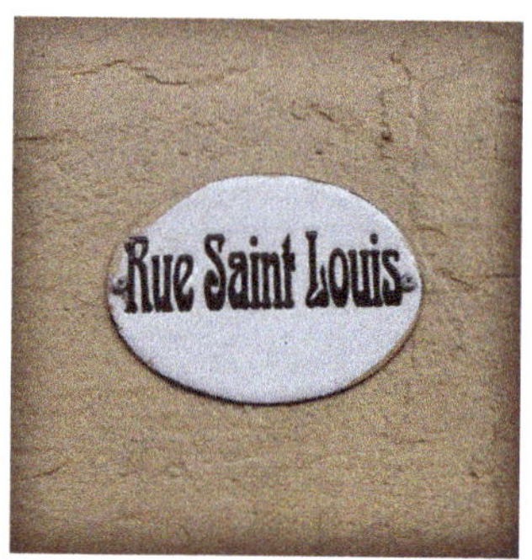

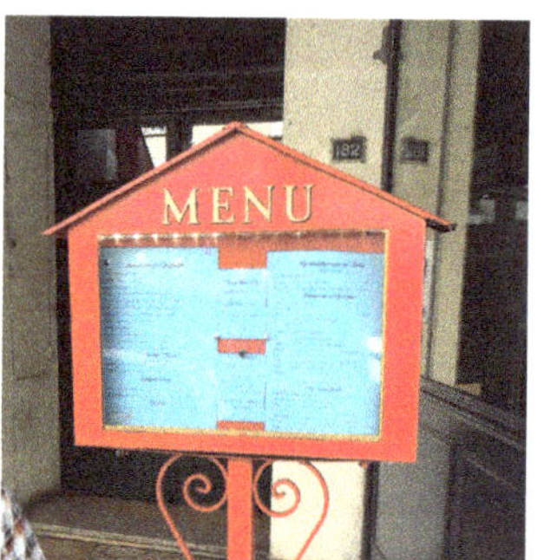

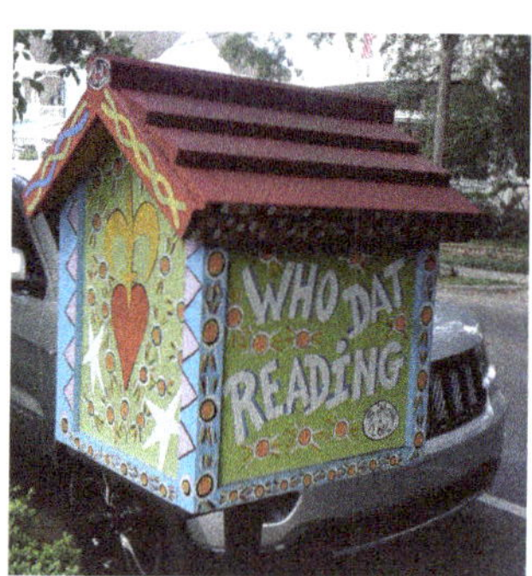

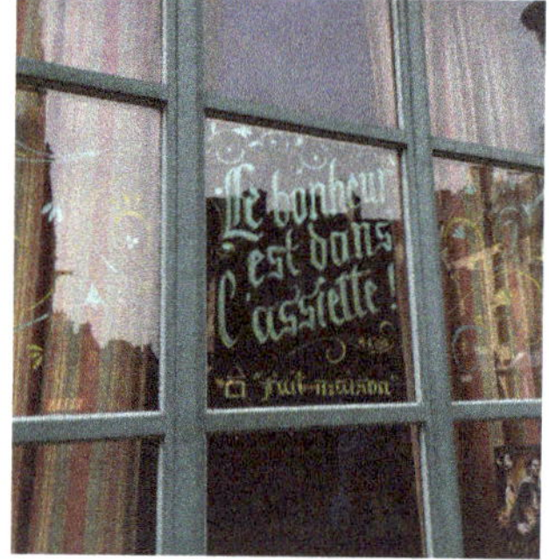

Creating, mark-making, and painting have all become a silent partner to me, holding their hand out to lift me up, saying, "Yes, girl, you got this! Keep on keeping on!"

~ **Patricia Coulter, Artist**

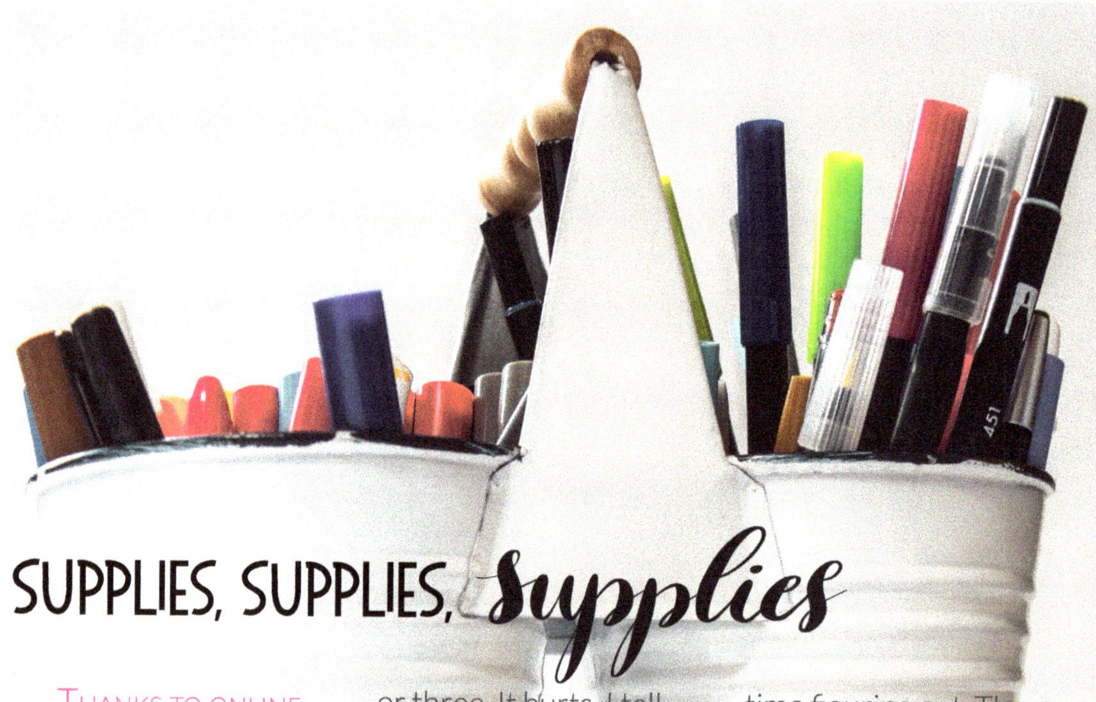

SUPPLIES, SUPPLIES, *Supplies*

THANKS TO ONLINE SHOPPING, IT'S MUCH EASIER TO GET YOUR HANDS ON THE LATEST AND GREATEST ART SUPPLIES.

But do you really need to spend a fortune? Not at all. You can make incredible art and lettering projects with the basics: a pencil, eraser, paper, and a few markers.

If you're like me, however, part of the joy of dabbling in artistic endeavors is trying out new art, lettering, and stationary supplies. I find it physically painful to walk out of an art or craft store without purchasing a wee, small thing, or two, or three. It hurts, I tell you. But with this great desire to spend funds on supplies comes great responsibility.

What if you accidentally damage a new (and costly) brush pen because you use it on the wrong paper? What if you grab the first marker you see only to discover – AFTER you wrote fancy welcome messages for your visiting sister across your front door – that the marker ISN'T water-based after all?

I call this the trial and error and error phase of any new hobby or skill and I know it well. Over the next few pages, I cover the supplies I've personally spent much time figuring out. There are still loads of products I haven't tried yet, but this compilation will give you a solid foundation of tools to start with and incorporate along your lettering journey. I do recommend you start small and gradually add to your artsy arsenal as your skills improve.

The projects included in this book are as low tech as I could make them, so that they can be created with either a basic amount of supplies or with more advanced products. Projects may require additional supplies or materials. Be sure to read the supply list sections carefully.

ele

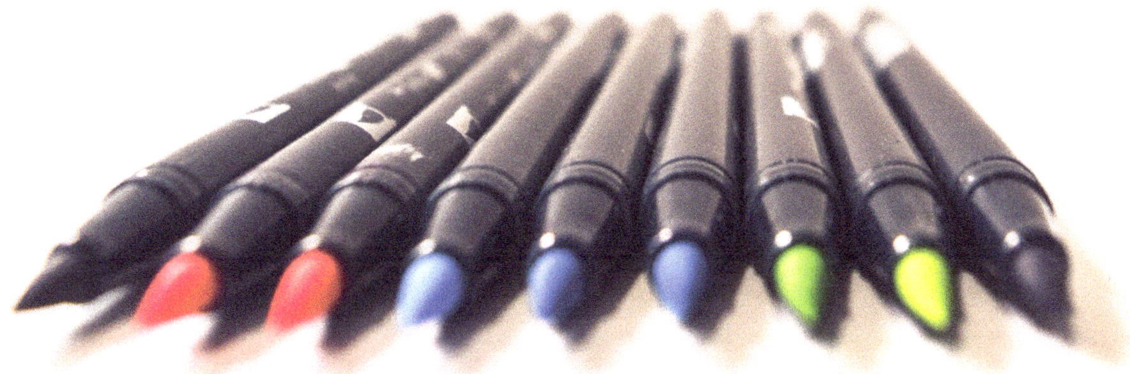

ALL THE CRAZY *beautiful* THINGS

Time to root through your crafting supplies, revist that old pencil case with the broken zipper and see what lovelies you already have kicking around the house. If you're fixing on a road trip to the nearest art or craft store, or are settling in to shop online, this information will be helpful.

BASIC *goodies*

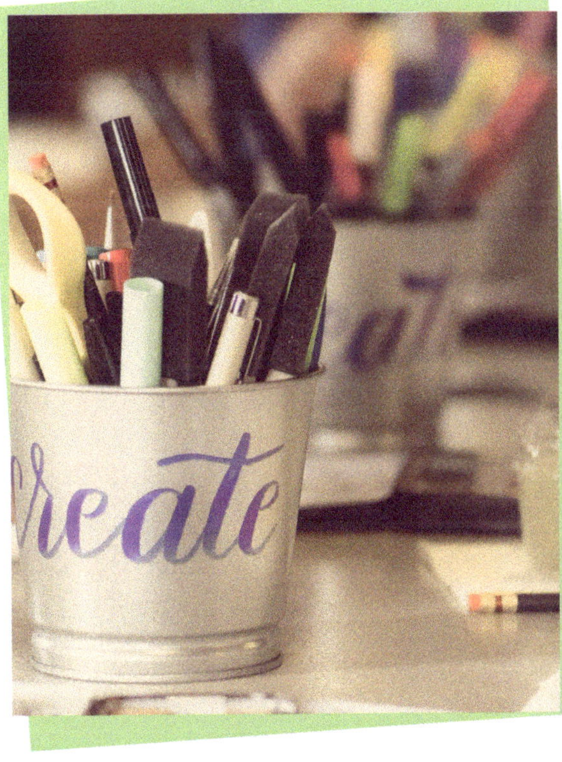

Pencil - I like to have a few types on hand. Mechanical, for quick sketches and finer lines (their leads tend to be lighter), regular HB for darker lines, and a graphite pencil for very dark lines and transfering designs. We'll discuss this on page 56.

Eraser - any will do, although white erasers tend to smudge less than traditional pink. Also, you can save time and a bit of mess if you use an absorbant kneaded eraser.

Scissors

Double-sided tape or glue stick

Painter's tape

Ruler or straight edge

Single hole punch

Paint brush - small and/or medium round tip for watercolour

Foam brushes - small or medium size as required for project

Brush Tips

Brush markers and pens may have large or small brush tips and there are a wide variety to choose from. My favourites are listed below.
(Be aware that some are water based and others are made with permanent inks.)

1. TOMBOW DUAL BRUSH MARKERS

These markers have a large, flexible brush tip at one end and a bullet tip at the other. Offered in a vast variety of colours, the water-based ink is the same hue from both ends. This enables seemless outlining or touchups. Tombow brush tips are meant for bigger lettering pieces. The flexible tip can be tricky to control at first.

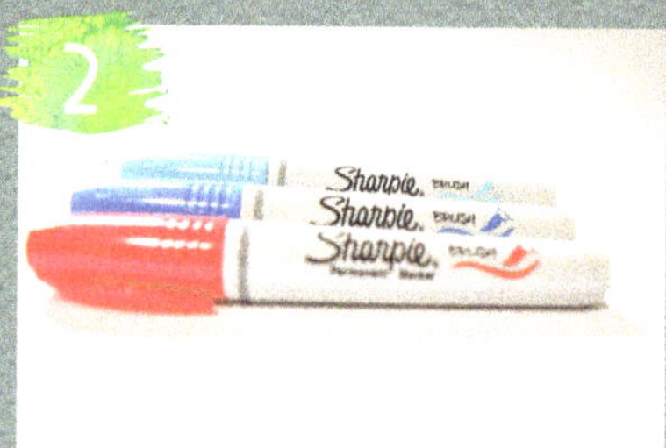

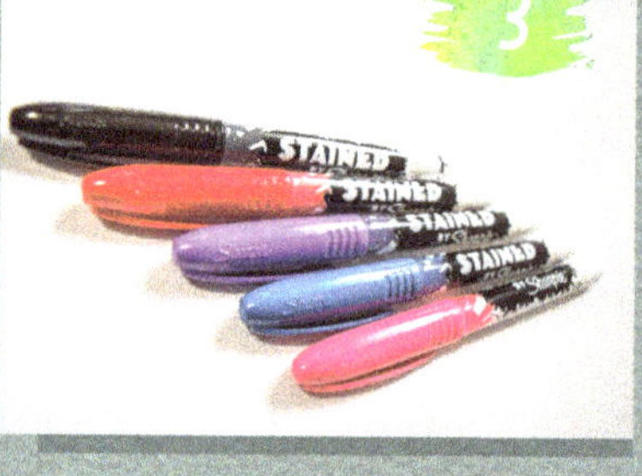

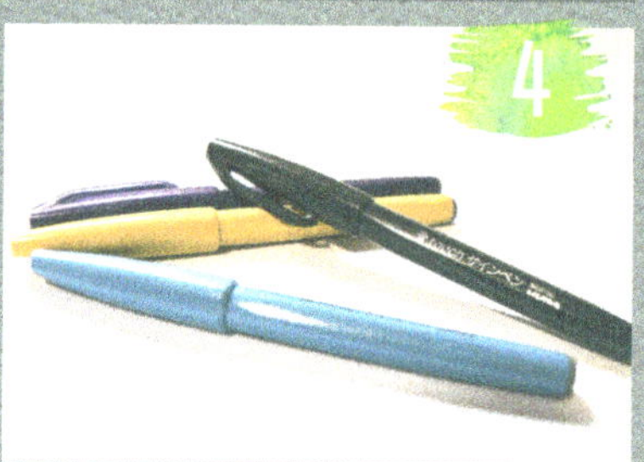

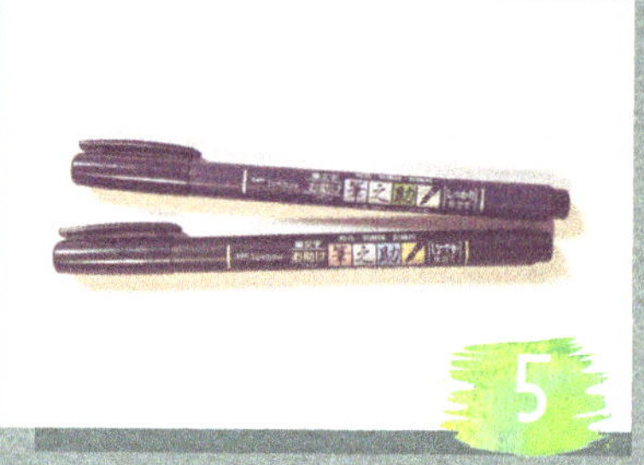

2. SHARPIE BRUSH MARKERS

Sporting a slightly smaller and thicker tip than the Tombow, these markers require a light hand to achive fine lines. The colour choice is minimal, but the ink is permanent, which gives you more surface options. These are able to mark on metal and are water resistant.

3. SHARPIE STAINED MARKERS

Although intended for marking on fabric, which they do a fantastic job of, I often use these on paper, cardboard, chipboard, or other surfaces because I am able to achieve a lot of control with this tip. The ink is permanent and may bleed through light weight paper.

4. PENTEL FUDE TOUCH SIGN PENS

This is my go-to pen for smaller lettering projects: envelopes, gift tags. The tip is small and flexible allowing for extremely fine lines combined with bold, thick downstrokes. Be sure to purchase the brush tip and not the firm bullet tip. The ink is water-based.

5. TOMBOW FUDENOSUKE

These are made with both hard and soft tips, so, again, be sure to aquire the correct one for your work. The soft tip is a bit firmer than the Pentel Touch pen, and might be easier to control for beginners. The hard tip functions as any other bullet tip pen. Ink is permanent.

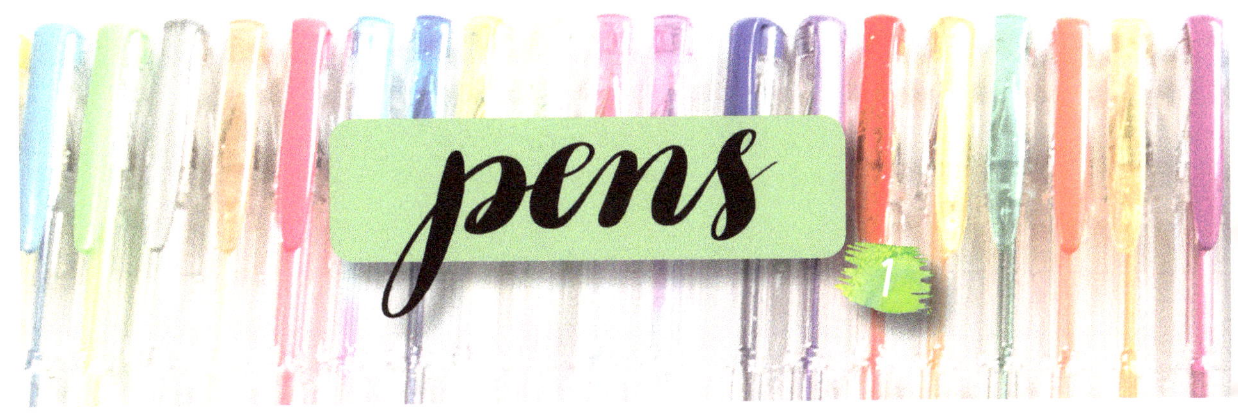

I find the terms "marker" and "pen" are often used interchangeably by manufacturers and artists alike. So don't stress if I'm refering to something as a pen, that you would instinctively refer to as a marker. As long as we both understand what the tool can do, it's all good. Here are a few of my favouite pens.

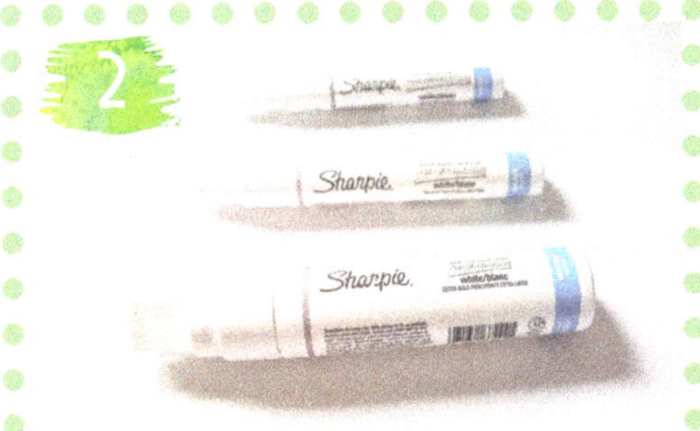

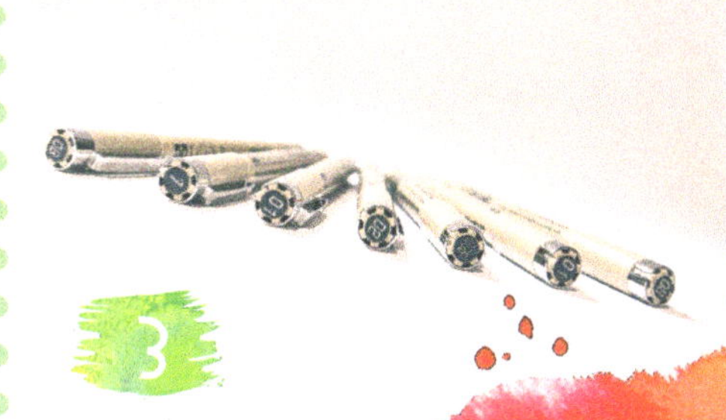

1. GEL PENS

These pens are divine for marking on dark paper surfaces, adding glitter or metallic details to art, or if you use a white gel pen, for adding highlights. Notorious for "not working", tips may need to be placed in warm water to reactivate the ink.

2 SHARPIE PAINT PENS

Keep your eyes on the end of these pens when purchasing. Water-based versions have a blue band and oil-based have red. It's important to note the difference as the oil based are permanent. I use the water-based pens to letter on chalkboard signs, wood, windows, and walls. The extra fine and extra points allow you to have a range of lettering sizes not possible with standard medium bullet tipped chalk markers.

3 MICRONS

Archival ink means zero bleed when you use these pens in-conjunction with watercolours. Available in super fine to brush tip. These are a favourite tool of illustrators and comic artists. Invest in a few sizes when you're ready.

Crayola broad and super tip markers are excellent and affordable options for lettering. I recommend investing in all the crazy beautiful colours!

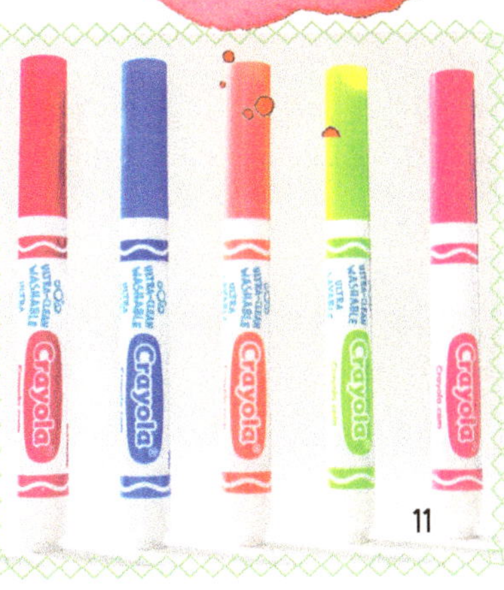

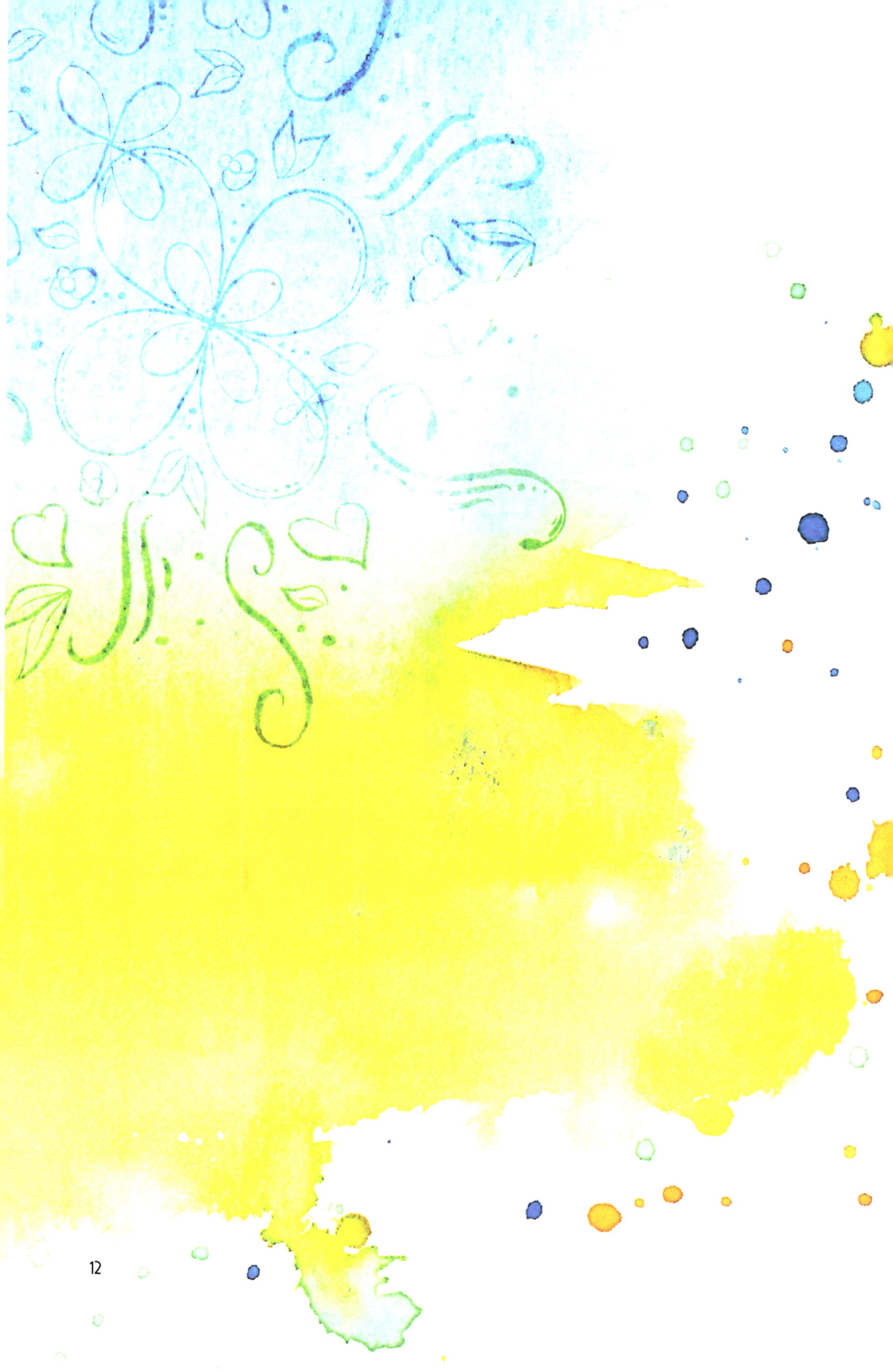

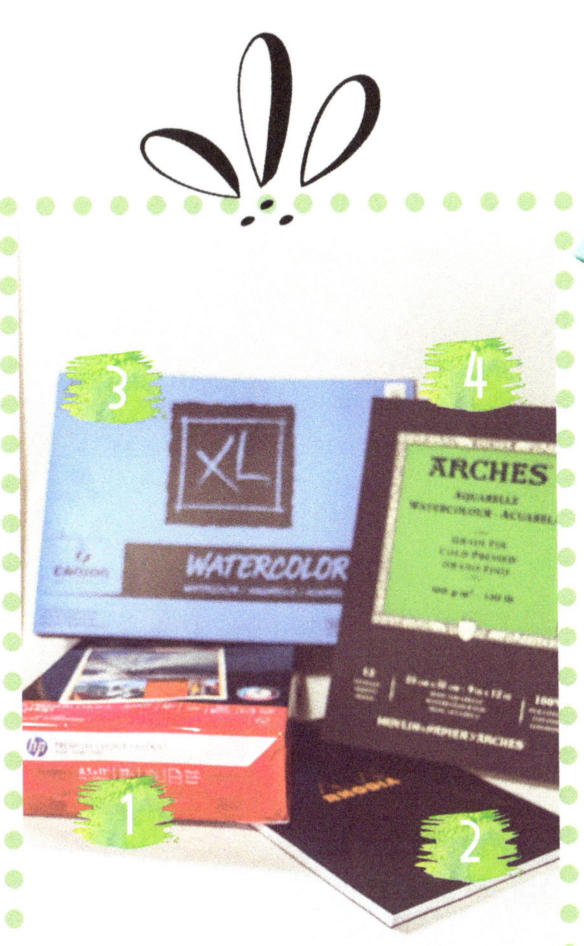

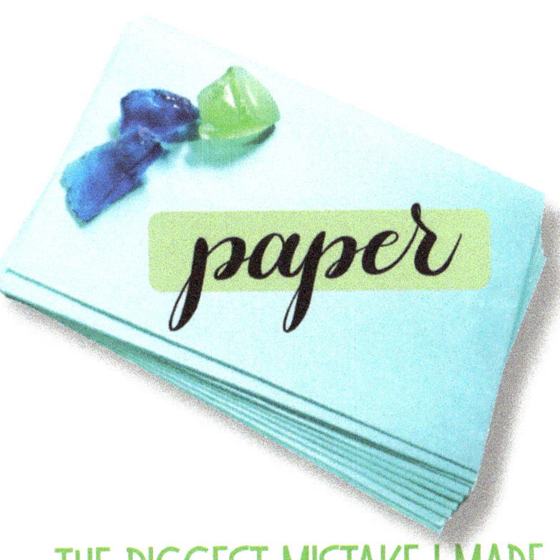

THE BIGGEST MISTAKE I MADE

as a beginning letterer was that I used the wrong paper, damaging most of the pens I initially purchased. A costly lesson and it's one of the first things I mention to students during my lettering workshops.

It deserves another font change:

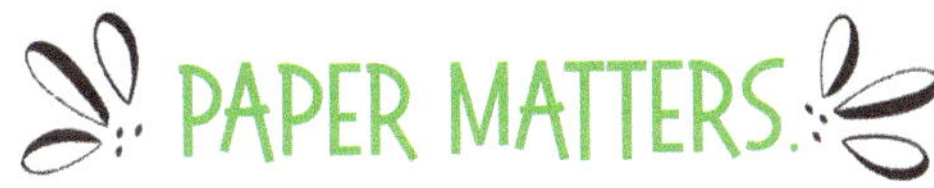

1. HP PREMIUM CHOICE LASERJET

This copier paper is a heavier weight than most and its ultra smooth surface makes it ideal for lettering. Comes in packs of 500 sheets and is a staple in my studio office.

2. RHODIA NOTEPADS

I'd never heard of these French notepads until I started getting serious about art. They've been around since the 1930s and it's easy to see why. The paper is superb for pen, marker, and ink. Notepads are available blank, with dots, or grids, and all have a perforated top for easy removal.

3. CANSON XL COLD PRESS

Watercolour paper comes in hot or cold press textures, and in variing weights (how much water it can hold before warping).

Cold press is more textured and allows for paints to flow and move on the paper. Hot press has a smooth, "ironed" kind of surface perfect for detail and controlling your paint. Personally, I prefer cold press as I enjoy the playful and often unexpected result as the water and paint dip and flow along the textured surface.

140 lb paper is the minimum weight you want to work with. The quality of your watercolour paper will dramatically affect your final product. Canson offers high quality at a great price.

4. ARCHES

More costly, as it is made to withstand more water than most, I reserve this paper for final watercolour pieces I intend to frame or give as gifts.

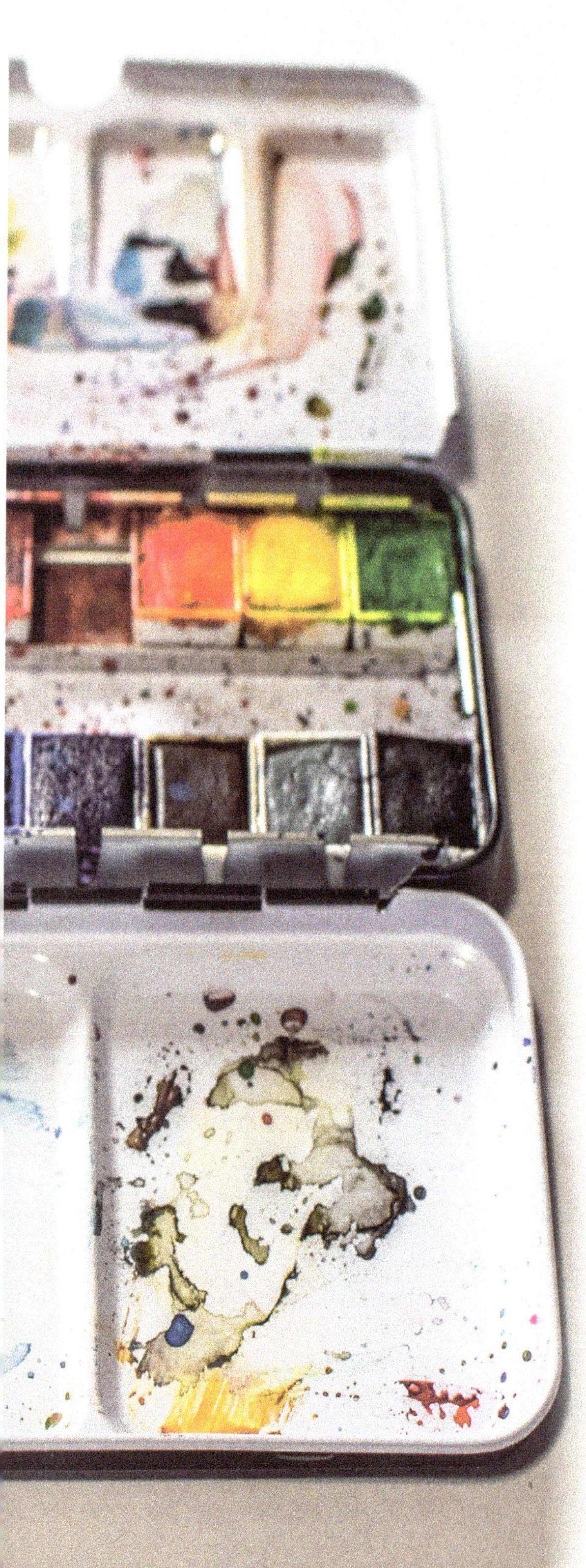

SCRATCH PAPER - It's also important to have scrap or scratch paper for working through your drafts, sketching and testing out design layouts. I use regular copier paper or graph paper for this purpose. Blank copier paper is great for freeflowing with your ideas and graph paper is useful for keeping things in proportion. **NOTE:** I would not use brush pens or markers on scratch paper as the surface is too rough and will quickly damage the tips.

TRACING PAPER - There are many uses for tracing paper, such as transfering designs from one surface to another, tracing over letterforms or practicing alphabets to build muscle memory to refining a sketch into a polished final design. Its smooth surface makes it an excellent option for lettering practice while using your brush pens or markers.

CARDSTOCK AND SCRAPBOOKING PAPER - These also can be solid options for lettering; however, be sure to get the ones designated as "smooth" surfaced, and not those with textures. Also be aware of those with a sheen or high gloss surface as you may need to use one of the permanent ink pens, rather than the water based.

ENVELOPES - Not all envelopes are created equal. Some are very thin and ink bleeds through them quite easily, others are thick and textured, requiring permanent ink markers.

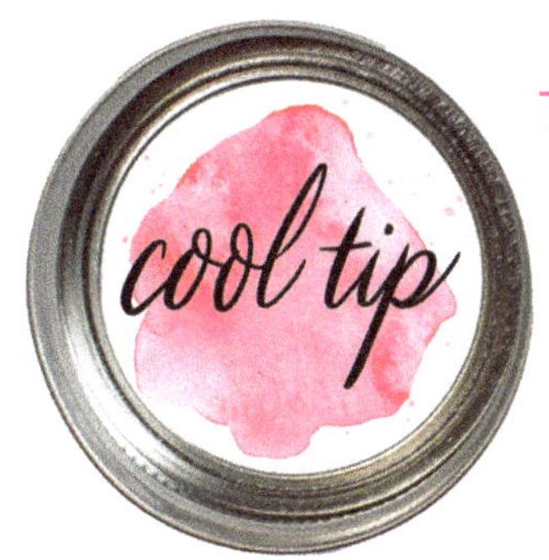

To prevent disappointment, I always do a quick test of paper and ink combinations before committing to the materials I'm going to use for a project. Got some new envelopes? Great! Use one as a tester and make marks with your various pens to see which will work best. Keep for future reference.

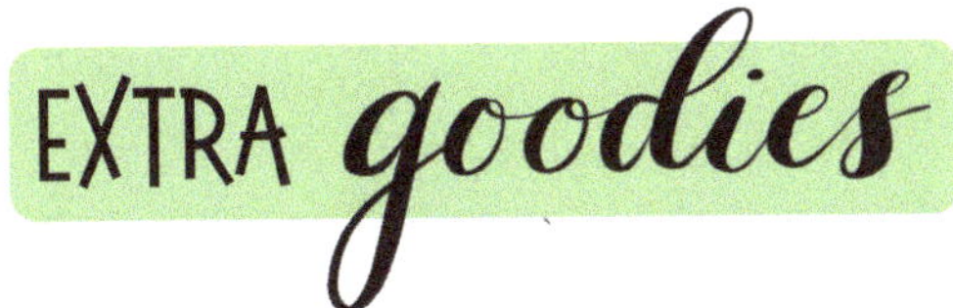

WATERCOLOUR - Several projects in this book feature watercolour elements. Watercolour and lettering are a match made-in-heaven sort of combination. These paints come in trays, tubes, and liquid concentrate forms. I suggest starting off with an inexpensive tray and working your way up to more expensive products. Be aware, however, that there is a noticible difference in the quality of the paints, colour vibrancy, how they blend on the paper...this is definately a case of you get what you pay for. I am a fan of any Winsor & Newton or Prima Marketing Inc. tray sets. But you can create beautiful pieces with watercolours of any form or cost.

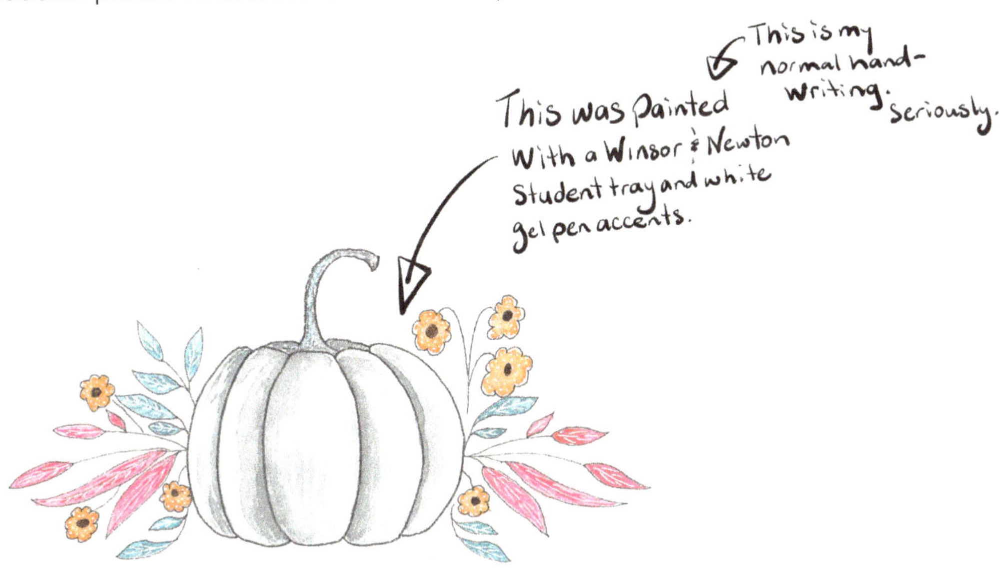

BLING - Ah, bling. This category refers to anything that can be used to accesorize paper. Often scrapbooking materials work well and come in infinite varieties and themes. Craft or dollar stores usually have loads to choose from: adhesive gems, stickers, small ribbon or paper flowers, laser cut wood shapes, press on bling – gems, butterflies, etc. My favourite bling is washi tape. Washi tape is crazy beautiful, but also can be functional - holding envelopes shut even as it acts as an embelish-ment.

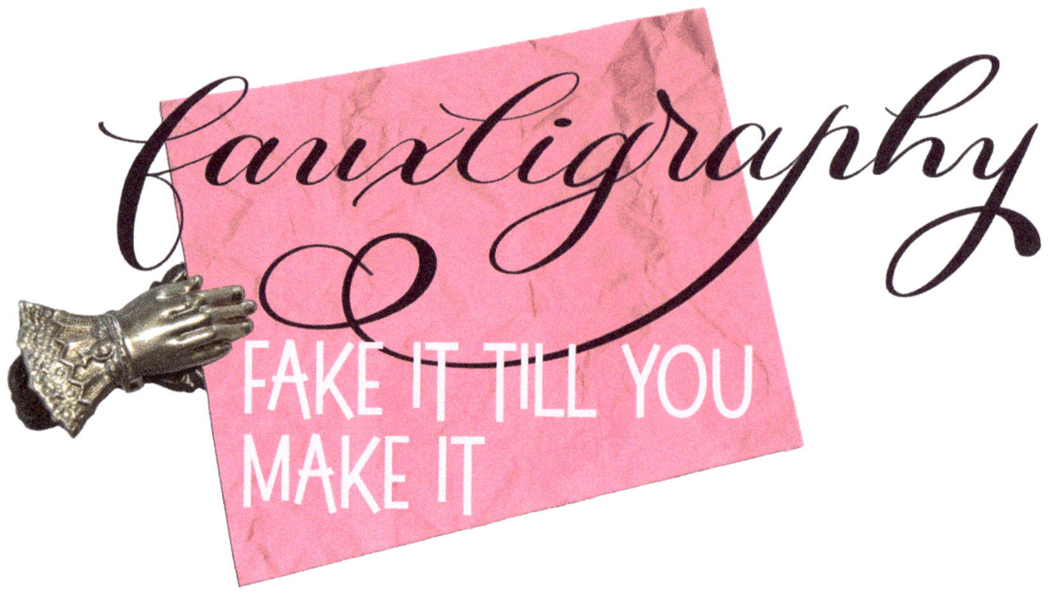

Calligraphy gets its trademark look from delicate, light pressure upstrokes, and thick, heavy pressure downstrokes produced by modern brush pens and, traditionally, pointed pens that are dipped in ink.

It does take time to develop control with brush pens and even when you have gained serious lettering chops, there will be times when you won't have access to the right tool. Or you might be working on an uneven surface, or you may want to write big - say, on a wall or a large window.

For these occasions, and for any time you want to add some drama to your writing with, even just a pencil, fauxligraphy is the way to go.

The examples on the next page will illustrate the steps I'm sharing with you to complete this "fake" or "faux" calligraphy look.

1. WRITE IN MONOLINE

When letting with a pencil, gel pen, ballpoint pen, or bullet tip marker, there is no variation in the line width you can produce. If you press harder, the width of your lettering will not increase, if you lighten your pressure, the line does not narrow. It's all the same. We call this writing in monoline. This is the first step in creating fauxligraphy.

2. ADD WEIGHT TO THE DOWNSTROKES

Remember, we're going for those thick "downs" and thin "ups". Since we can't do anything to change the thinness of the line, we're going to focus on the thickness. Add a parallel line to each downstroke, careful to follow the curves of your letters for a natural look. Keep the distance of your parallel lines consistent for your lettering to look polished.

1 fauxligraphy

2 fauxligraphy

3 fauxligraphy

4 fauxligraphy

3. FILL IN THE GAPS

Now that you have smooth lines to follow, it's easy to fill in the space between your original monoline and your parallel line. You can use the same pencil or pen to achieve a solid calligraphy look. For variations, you can fill the gap with lines, flowers, doodles, or simply a complementary colour.

That's all you need to start instantly creating beautiful letters!

4. BRUSH CALLIGRAPHY SAMPLE

For the sake of comparison, I've completed the same word, fauxligraphy, with a brush pen to show you the difference between fauxligraphy and actual brush lettering.

The major difference here is that it is faster to achieve this result with a brush pen. By using the flat side of the brush pen when you apply pressure on the downstrokes, you will make thick lines, and as you lighten pressure on the upstrokes and shift to the tip, the lines naturally narrow.

THINGS TO CONSIDER

In the grand scheme of things, remember to factor in a bit more time if you're using fauxligraphy.

You may also find it tricky to place the parallel lines. Do you add them to the inside, or the outside of the monoline? The answer to these questions depends on your spacing. If your letters are close together, you may have more room for the parallel lines on the inside. Or if your letters are nicely spaced out, you may have room on the outside. In a single word, you may alternate between the two.

This is how working with scratch paper or tracing paper can help you work out the kinks in your layout. You will be able to draw the rough idea and then tweak the spacing and placement as needed for a final draft.

In general, I space my letters out more than usual if I know I will be using the fauxlettering technique, so that I can stick with the majority of my parallel lines being on the outside.

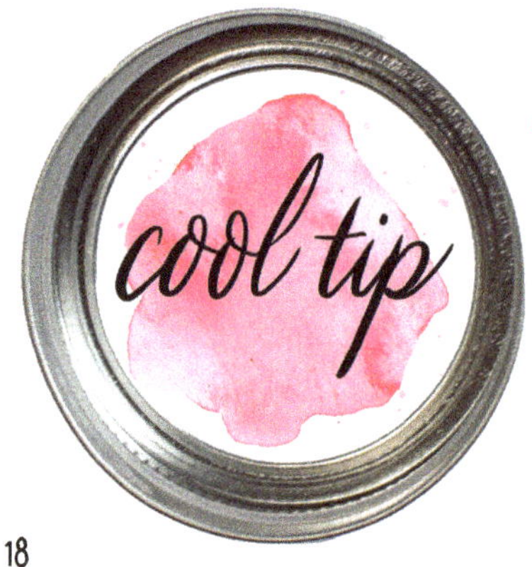

Adding weight to the downstrokes isn't a technique that only applies to cursive or flowing letters. Try writing your name in your regular printing and then follow the fauxligraphy steps to add weight to the downstrokes. How does this change the look? Vary how you fill in the gaps. Fun, right?

party
party
party

BEFORE WE DIVE IN

WE'RE ABOUT TO jump into the deep end with brush lettering, but there are a few housekeeping items to take care of before we start. The first is dealing with some common excuses as to why you won't succeed and the rest of the points on these two pages cover some lettering basics and lingo. Let's get to those good-old excuses.

FINDING TIME. CLAIMING YOUR SPACE.

BESIDES THE MONEY ISSUE, which we've addressed in the supplies section on page 8, the two most common excuses I hear from would-be letterers OR fiction writers, are, "But I don't have time...", or "I don't have space...". This is also where people tell me, "You have it easy because you don't have children and you have extra rooms in your house." It's true I don't have children, but I do have a husband, a part-time job, a writing career, an illustration and design company, dogs I adore, family, friends, laundry, yard work... And while I do have an office/studio in one of our spare rooms, the majority of the time (as my Instagram and Facebook feeds can attest) I work from my kitchen counter - the hub of our house. It's noisy, and busy, but I am at my most creative there.

My point is - if art, lettering, fiction writing, insert-your-dream-here, is important to you, you'll find time. Wake an hour earlier, stay up an hour later, skip that next episode on Netflix. Work in the livingroom, kitchen, or where ever you can. You can do this, if you really want to.

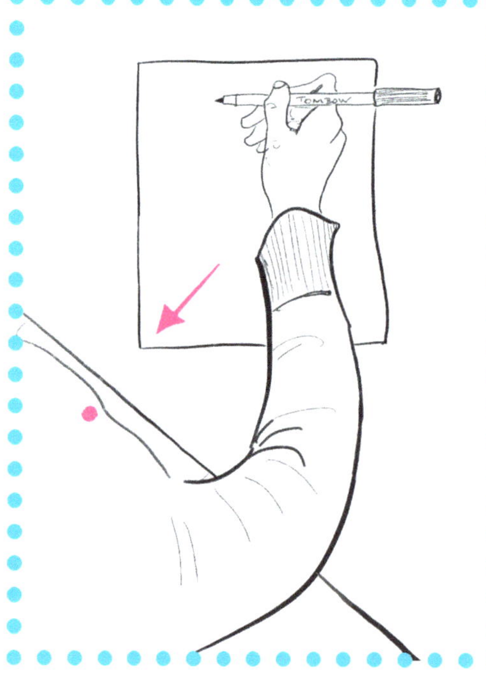

GUT INSTINCTS

It's important to tilt your paper so that the bottom corner is pointed directly at your solar phlexus, or as I like to call it, your gut.

This will help you instinctively establish a nice slant to your letters, as well as make it easier to hold your pen at the proper angle.

GUIDELINES AND WHY WE USE THEM

THE IMAGE BELOW shows my lettering on grid paper, but you should note the blue lines I've added with a maker and a ruler. These are guidelines I use to keep my lettering consistent. Often I will letter this way and then use tracing paper to create a final version once I'm happy with the work.

Even though brush lettering is known for its quirks and freeflowing look, there is still a need for guides, especially when practicing and learning. It's that whole, learn the rules before you break them deal. I have provided practice sheets within this book. You can photocopy these, or use tracing paper over them, or if you'd prefer to print them out, copies can be dowloaded from my website.

LETTERING TERMINOLOGY

ASCENDER LINE - The highest point for letter loops that ascend above the waistline.

DESCENDER LINE - The lowest point for letter loops that descend below the baseline.

BASE LINE - The line on which letters rest.

WAISTLINE - The highest point for lowercase letters.

X-HEIGHT – The space from baseline to waistline, usually the height of a lowercase "x".

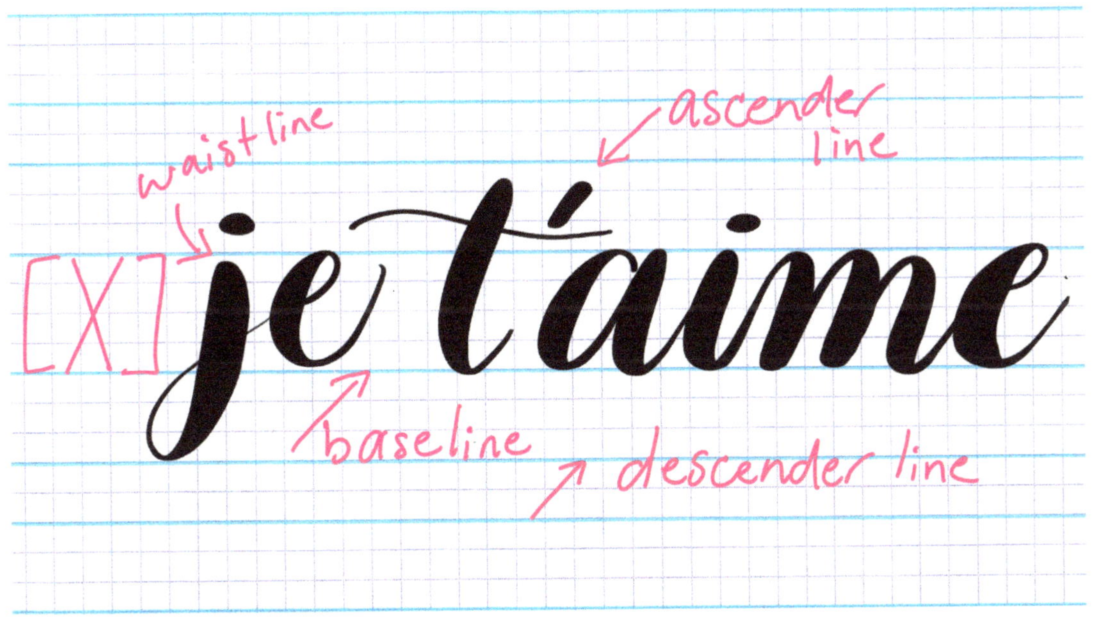

Let the pen skip and the ink run. When creating, there are no mistakes, only learning opportunities.

~ Megan Beaudoin, Artist

PROPER *grip*

Before we dig into the basics of brush lettering, there is one crucial aspect to address, how you grip your brush pen.

A brush pen can not be held as you would a pencil or a ballpoint pen, which is usually in an upright, "attack from the tip of the tip" position as with the first photo below.

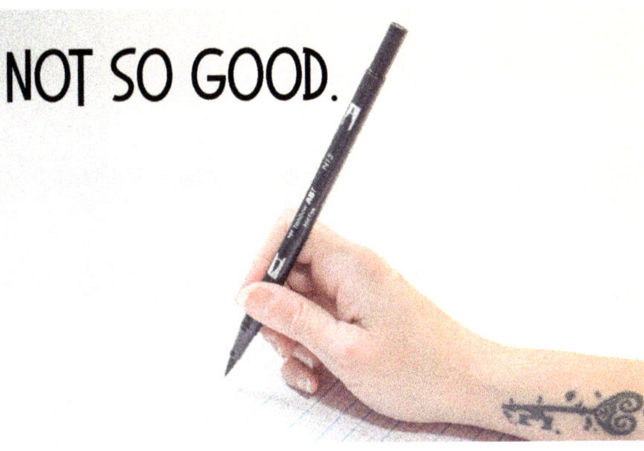

In this position it is impossible to achieve the thick downstrokes we're aiming for as the brush tip will not flatten to its full width.

Some people also tend to hold the pen too close to the tip which limits movement. The ideal grip is going to be different for everyone; however, there are several basics that will impact your lettering. The second photo, to the left, shows my ideal grip and I want you to give it a try, especially if you have been experiencing issues with thick and thin lines.

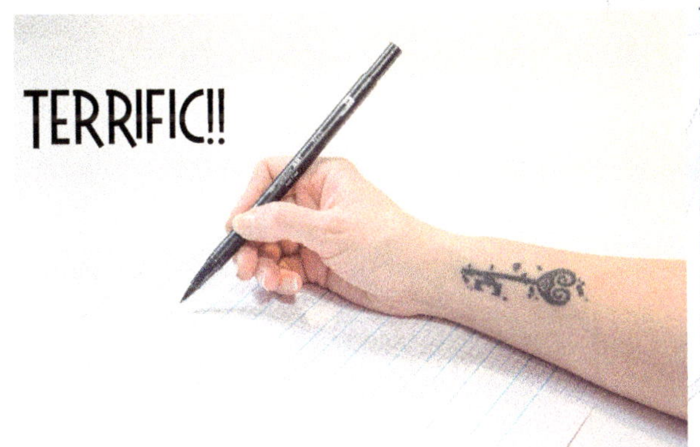

I am holding the pen at about 1.5 inches from the tip. I have my wrist tilted slightly and my pen is approaching the paper at a 45 degree angle, rather than a near 90 degrees as with the first photo. I am lightly resting the edge of my hand on the paper, ready to make large, flowing movements across the page.

basic STROKES

UPSTROKES - Start at the baseline and glide your brush pen to the waistline to create a light upstroke. When practicing these strokes, do at least one full row of each, striving for the same slant and even spacing.

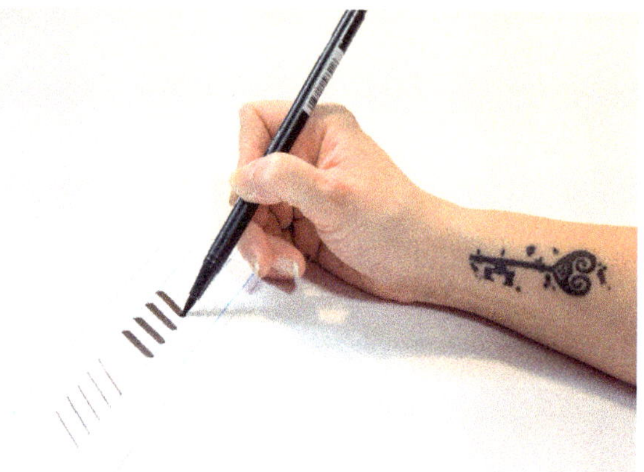

DOWNSTROKES - Start at the waistline and pull your brush pen toward yourself to create a thick downstoke. Watch your grip and let your hand slide down along your paper to achieve the thick downs. Your elbow may shift backward. This is normal. Don't try to make these shapes with just your fingers. The movement comes from your whole arm.

Don't worry if your lines are shaky or you find it difficult to achieve consistent spacing. These issues will be overcome with practice.

OVERTURNS - Start at the baseline with a light, thin upstroke and transition to a thick, weighted downstroke to the baseline. The goal here is to have a consistant arch at the top of each overturn. Not too pointy and not too square, an overall, incomplete oval shape is just right.

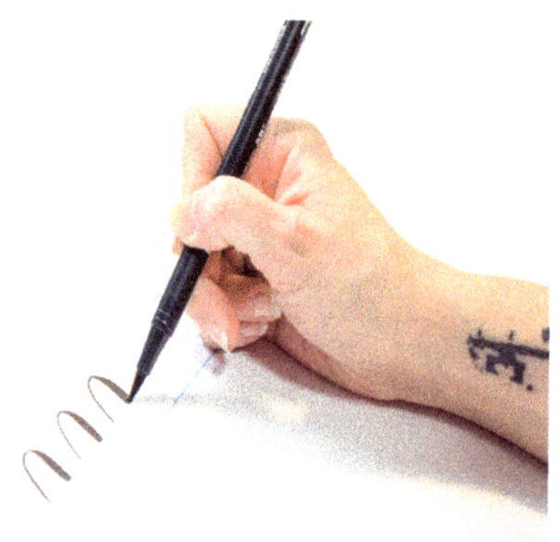

UNDERTURNS - Start at the waistline and pull your pen toward yourself in a thick downstroke and transition to a light, thin upstroke to the waistline. Again, aim for consistency with your arches and a gradual transition from thick to thin.

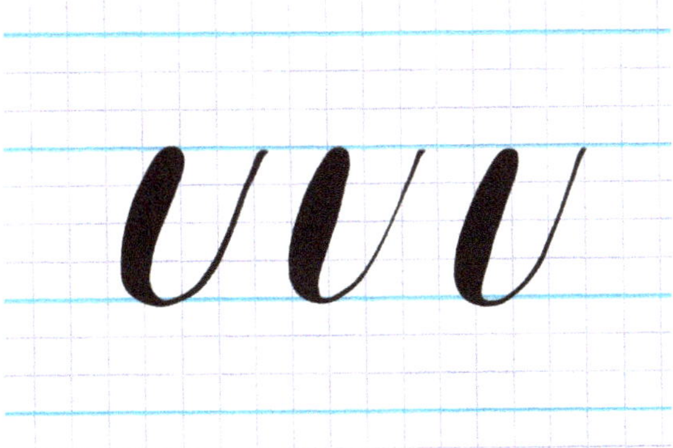

COMPOUND CURVES - This stroke combines the over and underturns in one smooth motion. Start at the baseline with an upstroke to the waistline, transition to a thick downstroke to the baseline, and follow through with another upstroke to the waistline. The key here is to have equal width across both turns and similar arches.

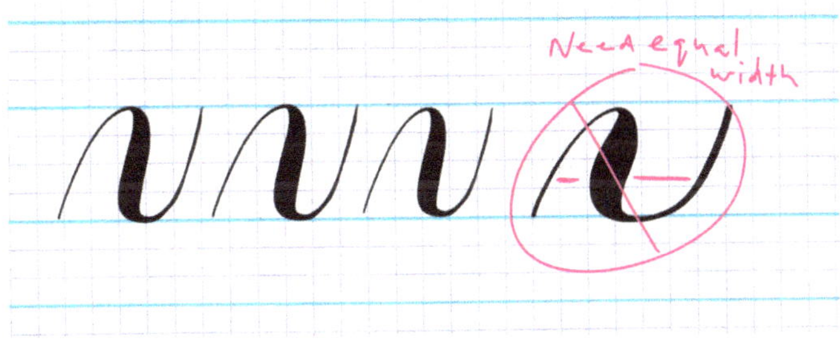

ASCENDER LOOPS - Start at the waistline with an upstroke to the ascender line that curves counterclockwise into a thick downstroke all the way to the baseline. This will be the loops for our “b”,s “f”s, “h”s, “k”s, and “l”s.

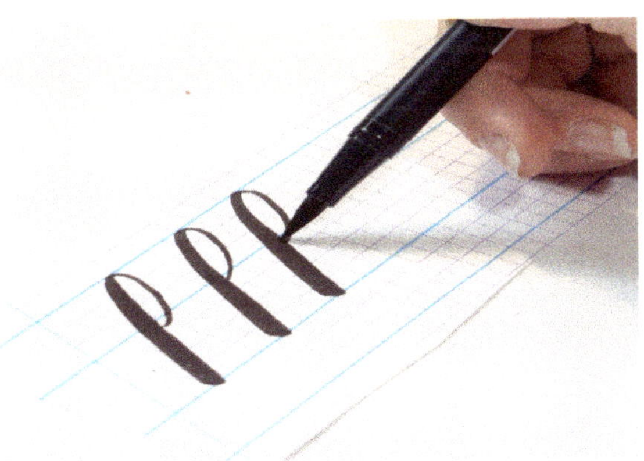

DESCENDER LOOPS - Start at the waistline with a downstroke all the way to the descender line and curve clockwise in an upstroke to the baseline. This will be the loops for our "g"s, "j"s, "p"s, "y"s, "z"s.

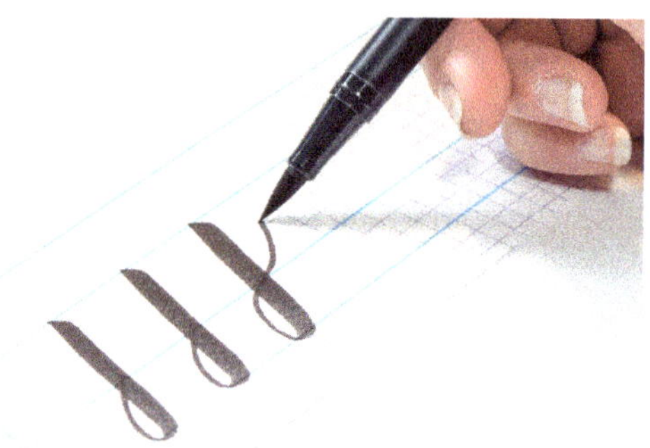

OVALS AND REVERSE OVALS - Possibly the most important stroke to learn, the oval is the basis for our lettering alphabets. However wide or pointy or rounded we make our ovals, the other letters will take a similar shape as so many incorporate this stroke. Start on the right and with a light upstroke, move in a counterclockwise direction to a thick downstroke and transition back to a light upstroke, meeting your original startoff point.

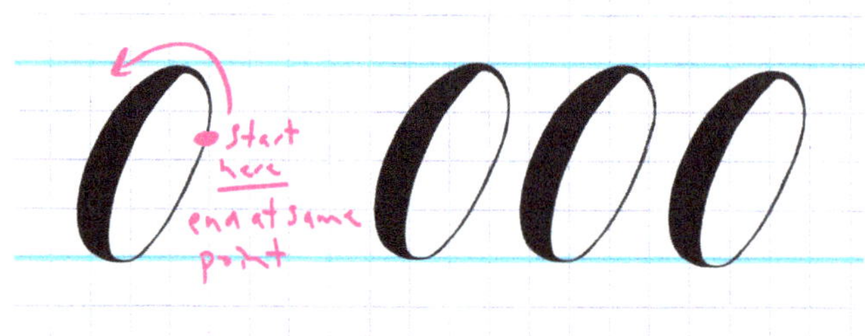

Learn to create ovals in both directions. These reverse ovals will be used for our "b"s, "p"s, and are useful for flourishing.

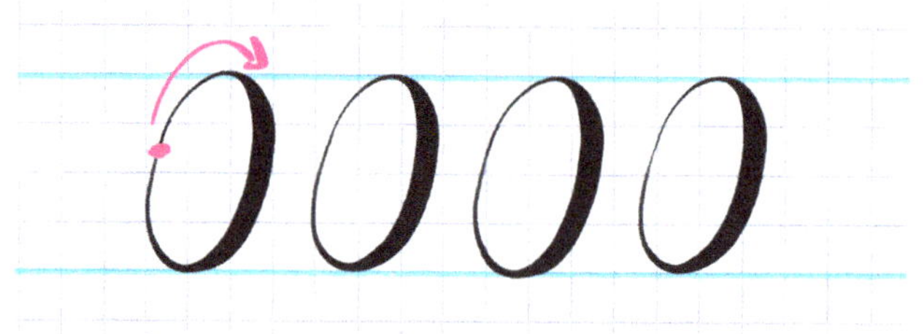

GIVE IT A GO - It's time to practice. Using tracing paper on top of the practice guides I've provided. Once my marks run out, continue to add strokes on your own to complete the line. You can do this as many times as needed to build skills.

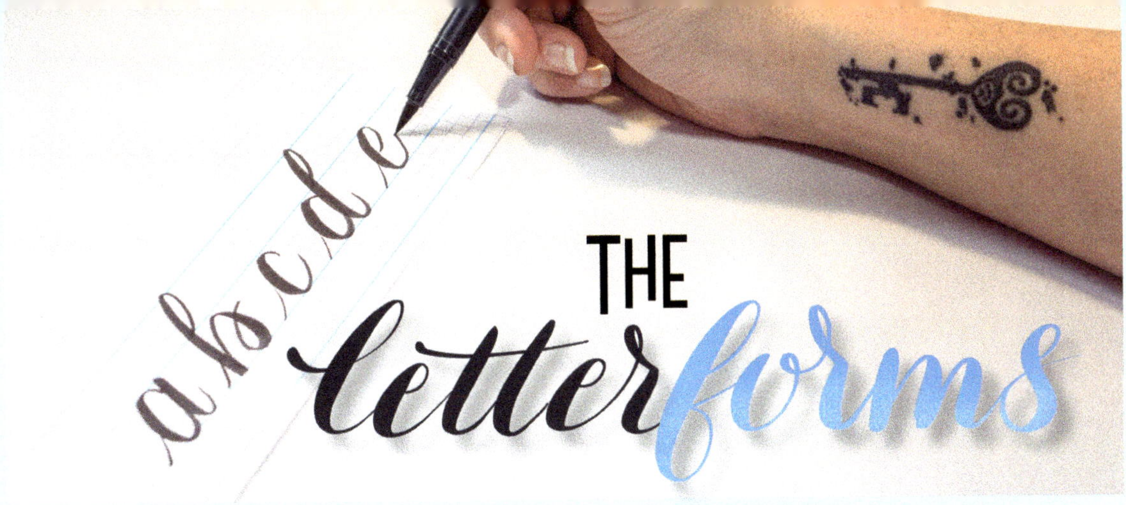

THE letterforms

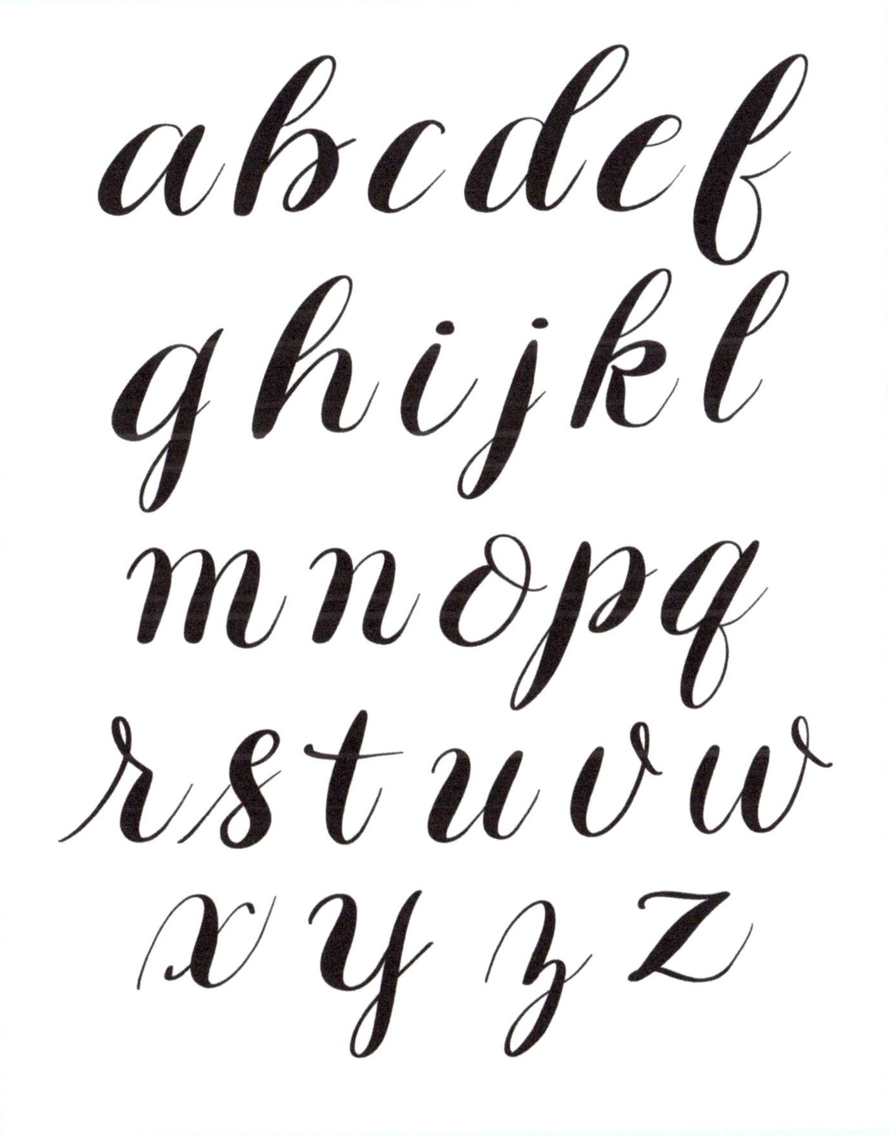

a b c d e f

g h i j k l

m n o p q

r s t u v w

x y z z

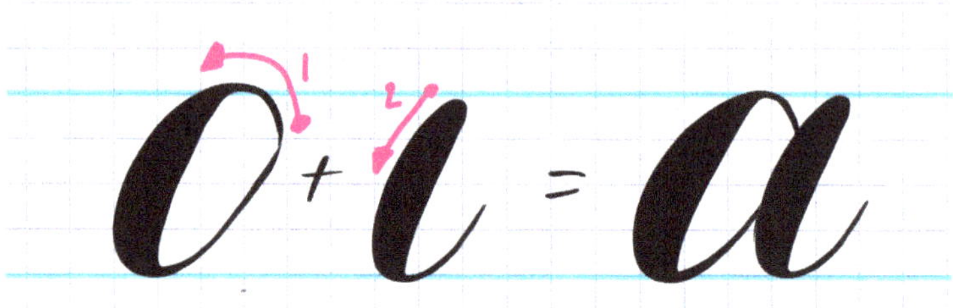

Here we go! You'll quickly see how important it is to practice the previous foundational strokes as all letters are made from them in various combinations. The lowercase "a" consists of an oval and a partial underturn. That last upstroke doesn't come all the way to the waistline.

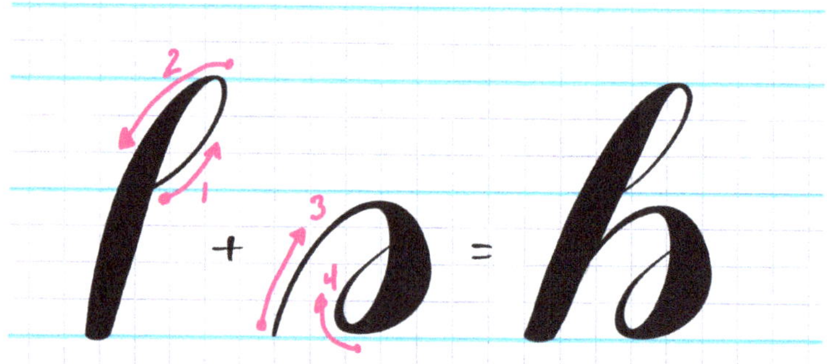

The lowercase "b" consists of an ascender loop and reverse oval or an overturn if you prefer to think of it that way. The trick here is to keep a similar oval shape for all your letters within a particular style. For example, your lowercase "b" should take up the same width as your lowercase "a", although, of course, it will be taller.

c = easy, right?!

Again, the lowercase "c" is essentially an incomplete oval. Remember to keep the same slant with all your letters and keep a clear "thick" and "thin" with this shape. Start with a light upstroke, progress to a thick downstroke and transition to another light upstroke.

Practice time! Photocopy this page onto quality paper or place tracing paper over top and letter from there. Note that in all of these examples, I'm not lettering on regular graph paper. These are sheets from a Rhodia grid paper notebook. You can use regular graph paper, but ONLY under tracing paper so you do not destroy your brush tips.

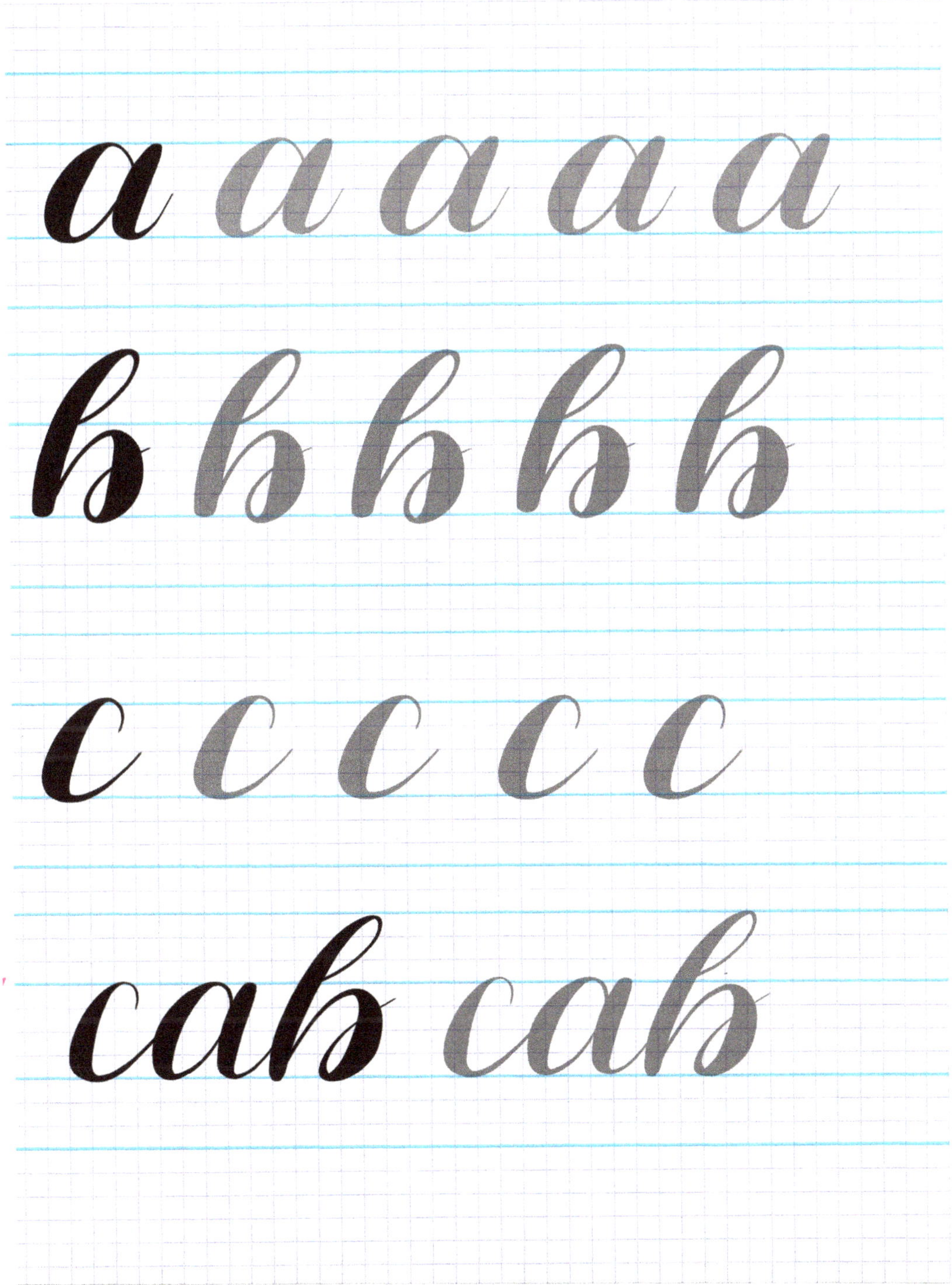

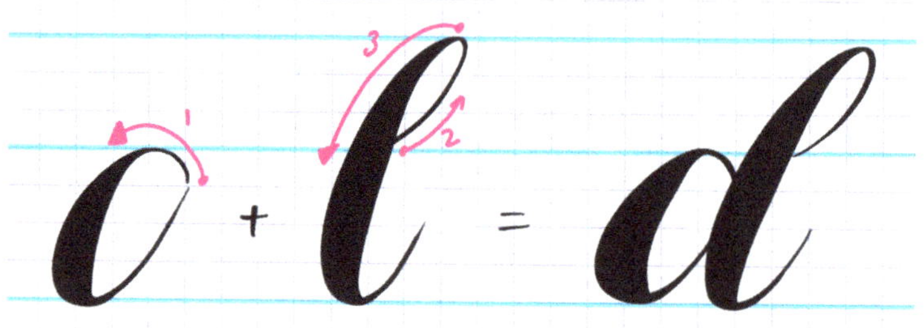

The lowercase "d" consists of an oval and an ascender loop. I know it's tricky, but try to keep all your ascender and descender loops as close to the same width and shape as possible. This will ensure your letters look like they belong together. It's fun to exaggerate loops and dips, but consistency is important when you're just starting out. If you're just starting out, there are so many elements to think about: your brush grip, your lettering slant, your posture ... let's keep with the less is more frame of mind for a while.

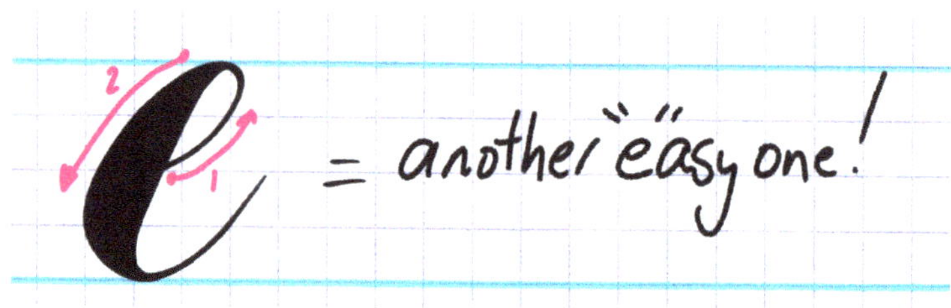

The lowercase "e" consists of another incomple oval, or a squished ascender loop.

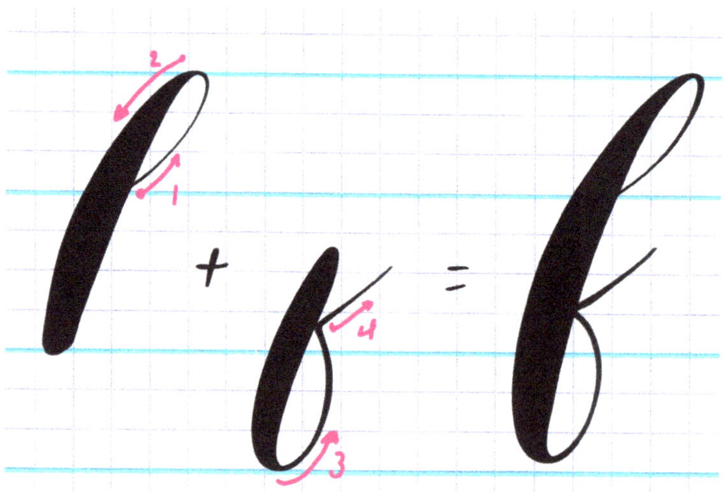

The lowercase "f" is the longest letterform in the bunch. It consists of an ascender loop and a descender loop that exits to the right, rather than the left.

d d d d d

e e e e e

f f f f f

fade fade

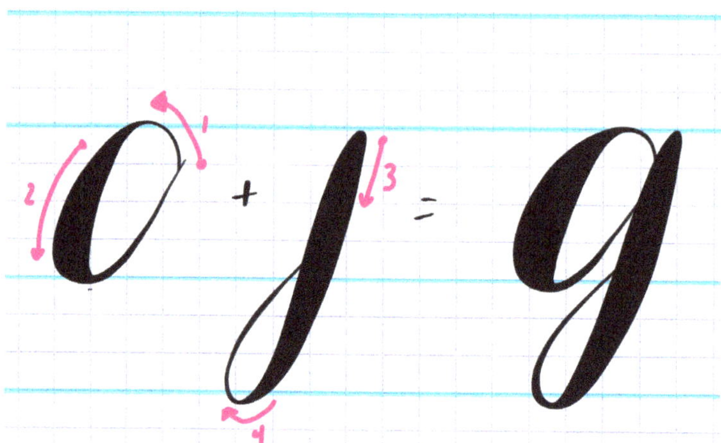

The lowercase "g" consists of an oval and a descender loop. How are your oval shapes when you do a "g", a "b", an "a" and a "c" together, one after another on the same line? Do they look fairly consistent? Could all of the ovals sit on top of each other and take up the same amount of space?

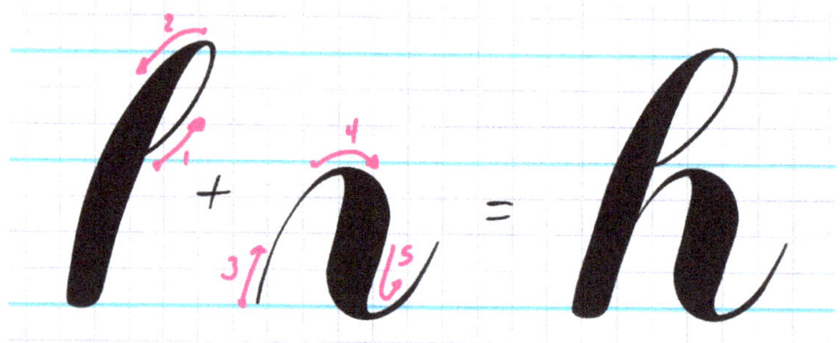

The lowercase "h" consists of an ascender loop and a compound curve. This is one of my favourite letters.

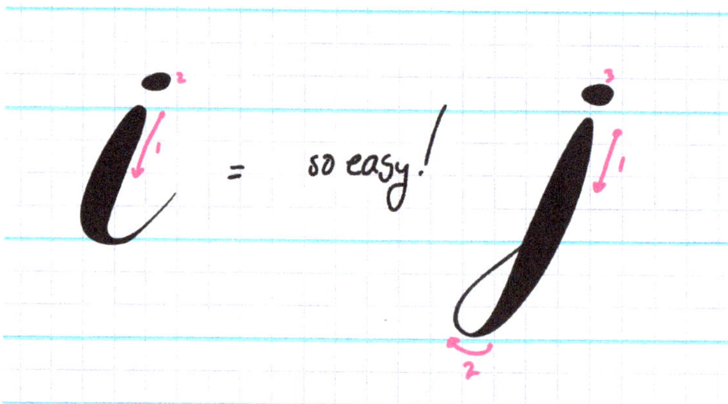

The lowercase "i" and "j" are quite similar. Be sure to keep your dots centered over the downstrokes and just above the waistline.

g g g g g

h h h h h

i i i i i

j j j j j

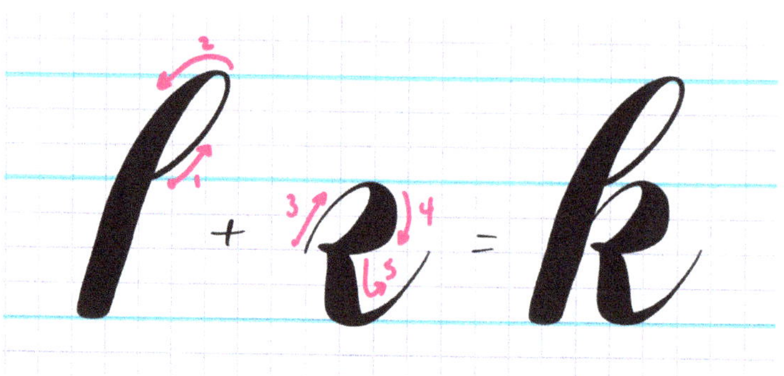

The lowercase “k” consists of an ascender loop and a unique shape that resembles an “r” or a tear drop formation that moves to an underturn. This letter is my nemesis. It took me a long time to build the required muscle memory. It’s normal to find some letterforms more challenging that others. When you encounter this, do NOT avoid the letter. In fact, practice it more than any other until you are comfortable.

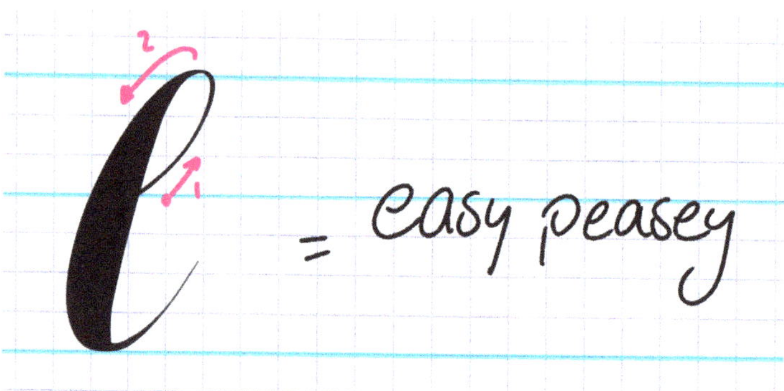

The lowercase “l” consists of an ascender loop and a smidge of an underturn.

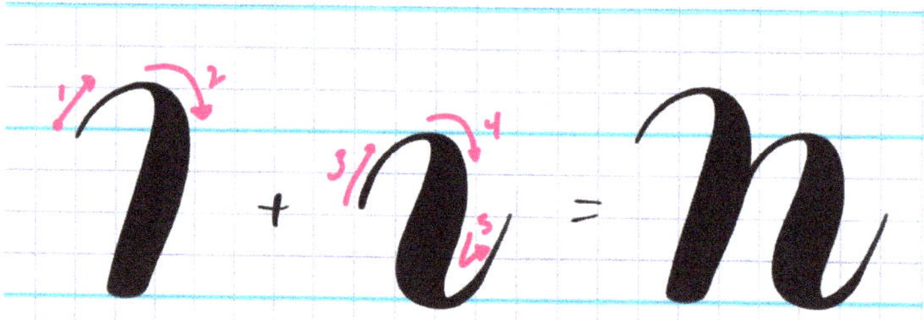

I know this isn’t in alphabetical order, but let’s learn the “n” first as an “m” is just more of the same. The lowercase “n” consists of a downstroke and a compound curve. I like to have a bit of an arch or small overturn at the start of the downstroke, but you could do a simple downstroke right from the waistline, without the little arch.

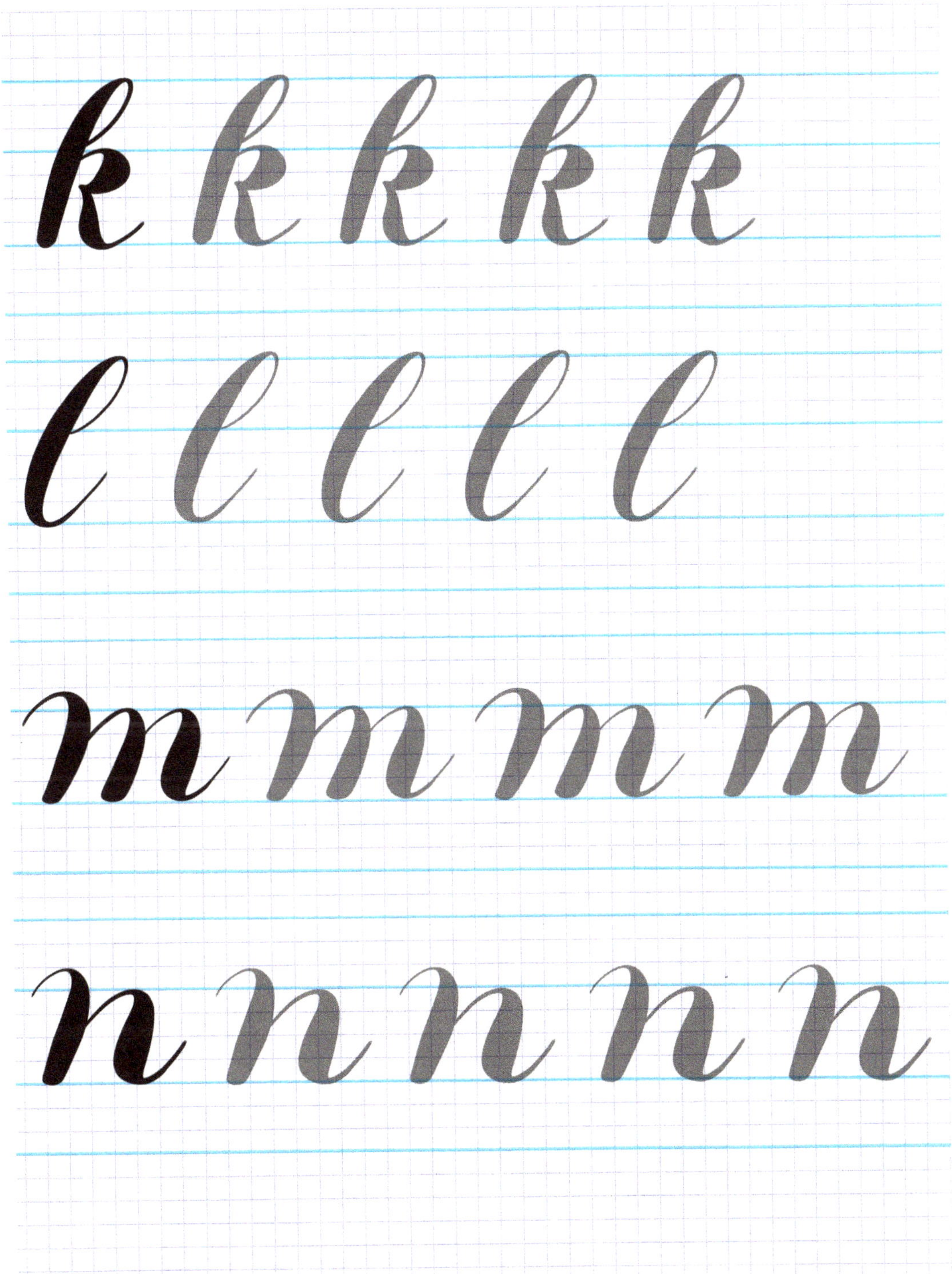

k k k k k

l l l l l

m m m m

n n n n n

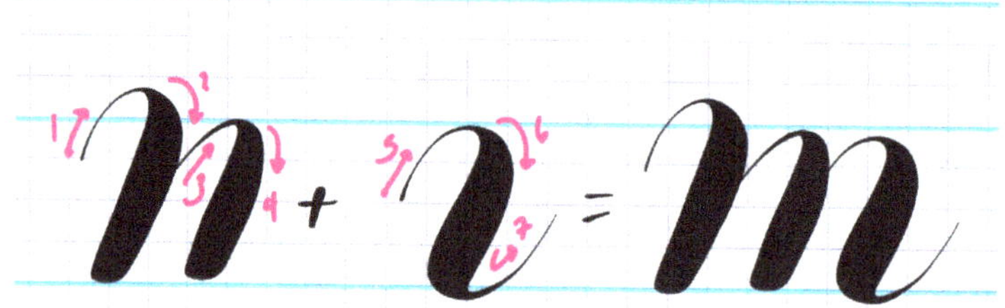

The lowercase "m" consists of a downstroke, an overturn, and a compound curve. As with the "n", I like to have a bit of an arch or small overturn at the start of the downstroke, but you could do a simple downstroke right from the waistline, without the little arch. Aim for consistent arches and a consistent slant throughout this letter. All the downstrokes should be parallel lines.

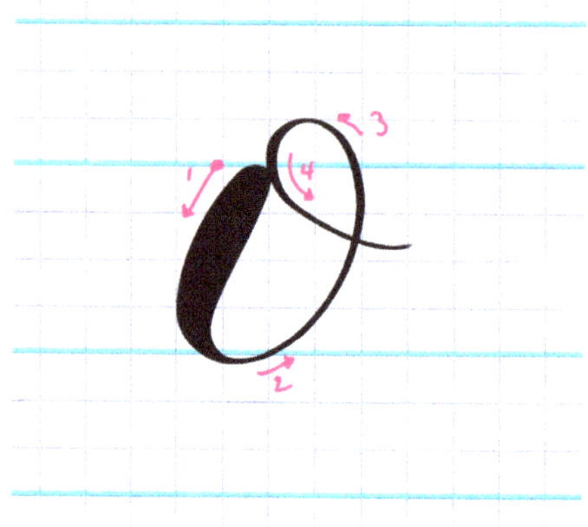

The lowercase "o" consists of an oval. In this example, which is my go-to "o", I've added a loop at the top that exits to the right for smooth transition to the next letter.

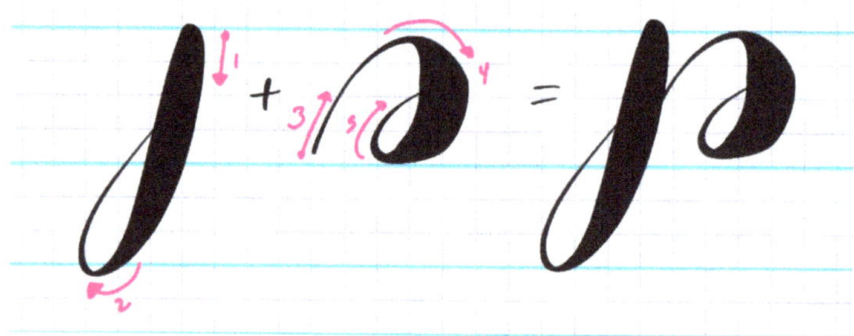

The lowercase "p" consists of a descender loop and a reverse oval or an overturn. In this example, my reverse oval doesn't touch the downstroke. It's fine if you completely close the oval and follow through with your exit stroke to the right. Either way works.

o o o o o o o

p p p p p p

hope hope

look look

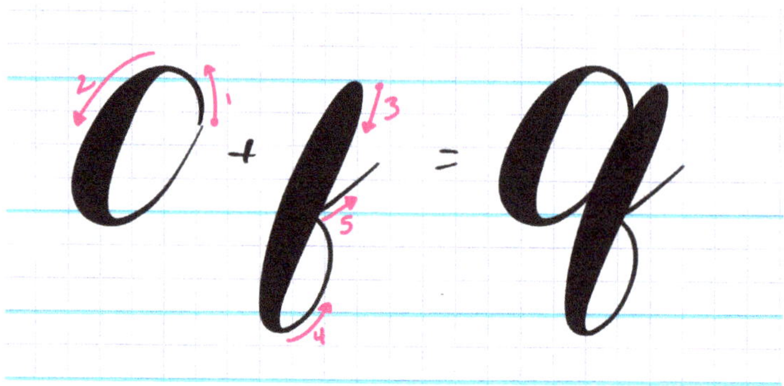

The lowercase “q” consists of an oval and the same descender from the lowercase “f” which exits to the right, rather than the left.

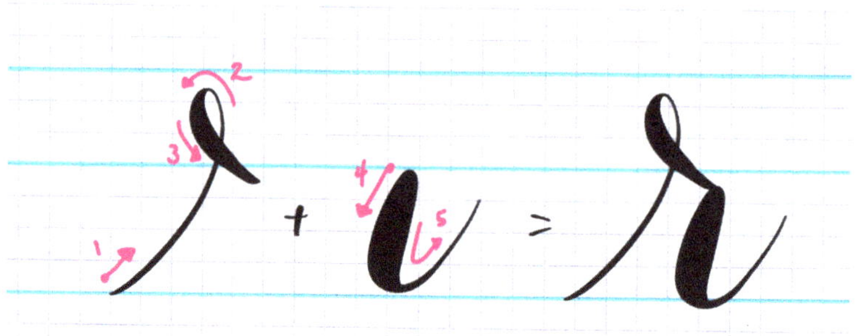

The lowercase “r” and “s”, below, are unique in that they have some unusual shapes thrown into the mix and they both ascend slightly above the waistline. The “r” consists of an entrance stroke that crosses the waistline, loops and slices down through the waistline again, along with an underturn.

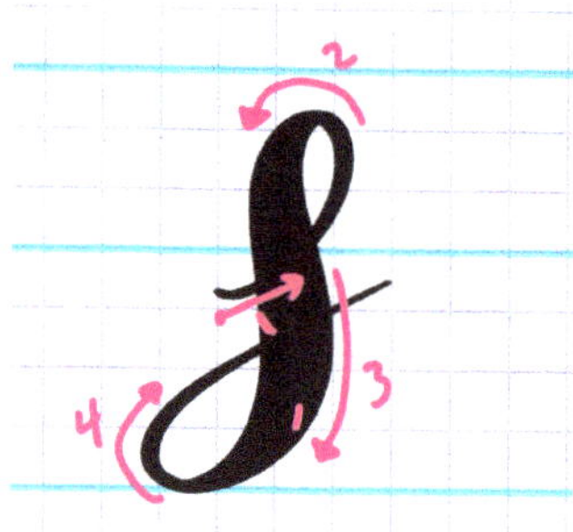

The lowercase “s” consists of an entrance stroke near the waistline that moves upward to cross the waistline, loops into a curved and shortened descender loop shape that comes back up to the waistline.

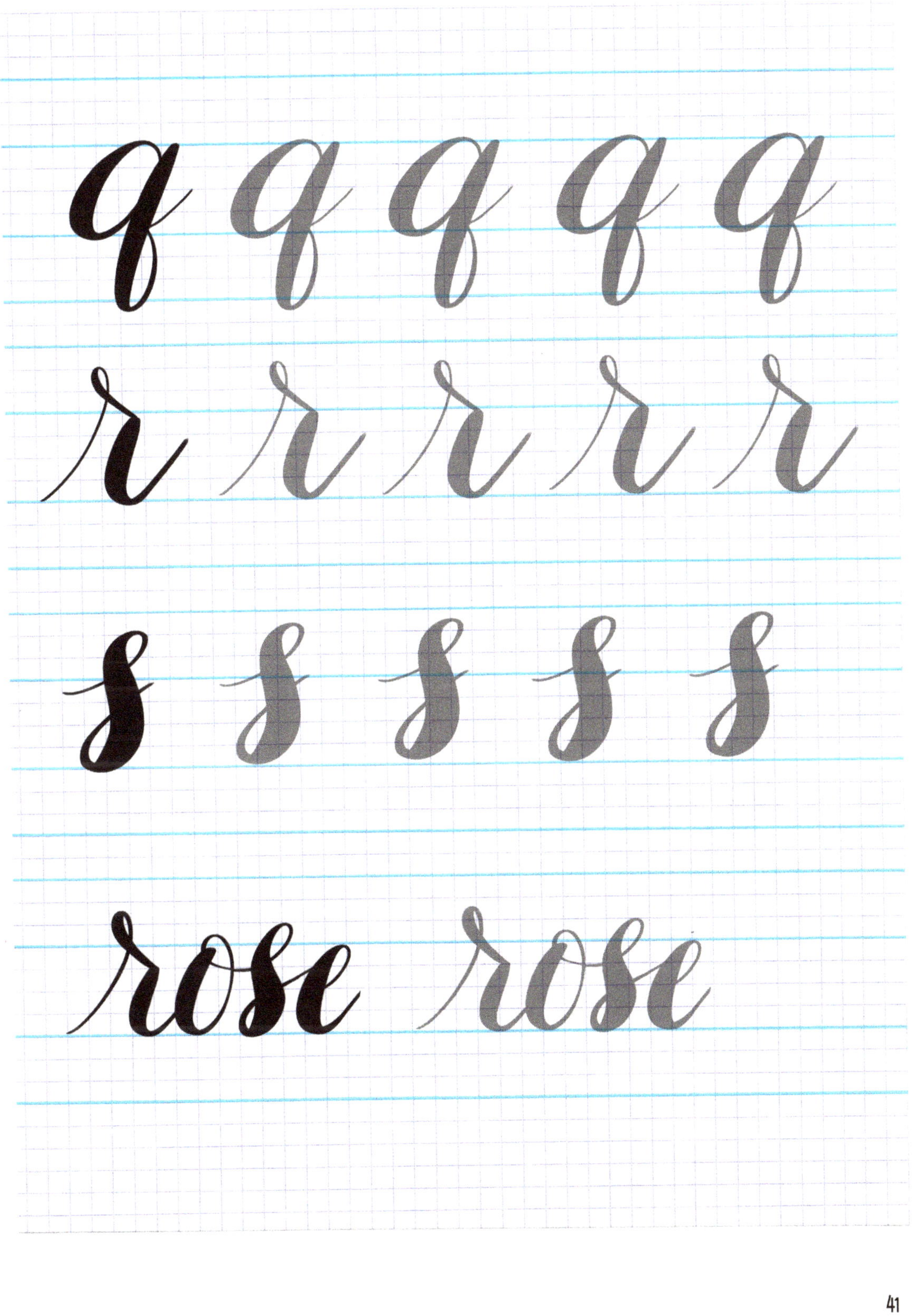

q q q q q

r r r r r

s s s s s

rose rose

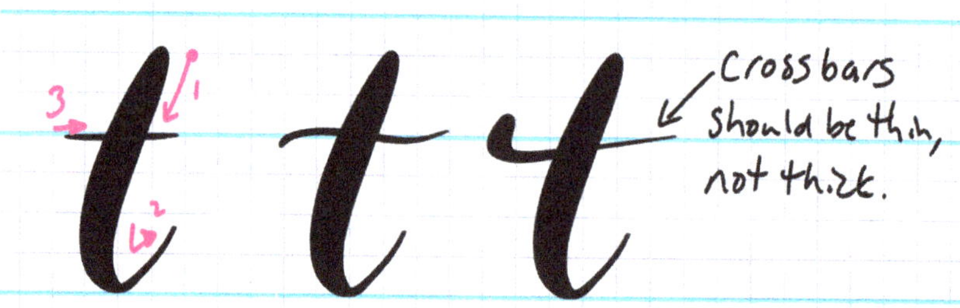

The lowercase "t" consists of a downstroke that starts above the waistline but not all the way to the ascender line, a mini underturn and a crossbar. The crossbar offers a prime location to add some flare or keep the letter controlled. But no matter how you make your crossbar, it should be far thinner than the downstroke or the letter loses it's flowing grace.

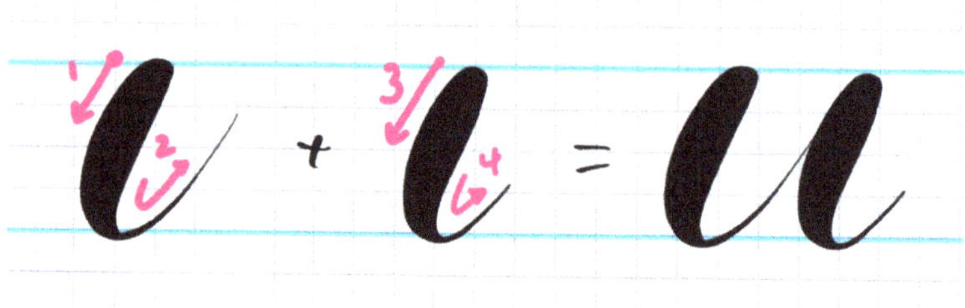

The lowercase "u" consists of a full underturn, followed by a partial underturn. As with the lowercase "n" and "m", you could add an arch at the top of the downstroke. So to with the "v" and "w" below.

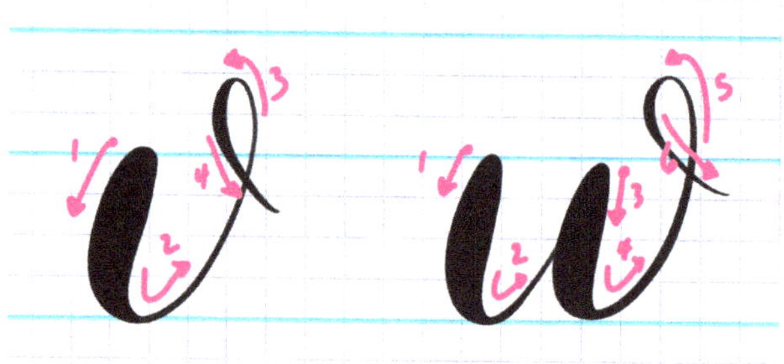

The lowercase "v" and "w" are very similar. The "v" consists of an underturn with a little loop at the end. The "w" consists of a full underturn, followed by the "v" form.

t t t t t

u u u u u

v v v v v

trust trust

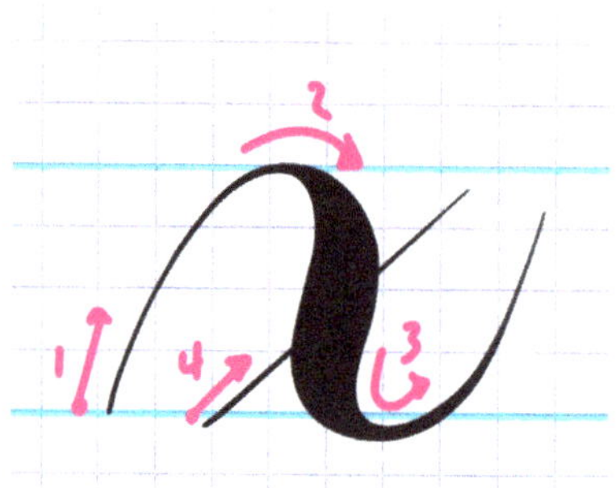

The lowercase "x" consists of a compound curve and cute, if random (and thin!) line that bisects the downstroke at an angle all its own. You may have to play around with the exact placement of that line for one that matches your style. Once you've found your sweet spot, just keep it consistent when practicing.

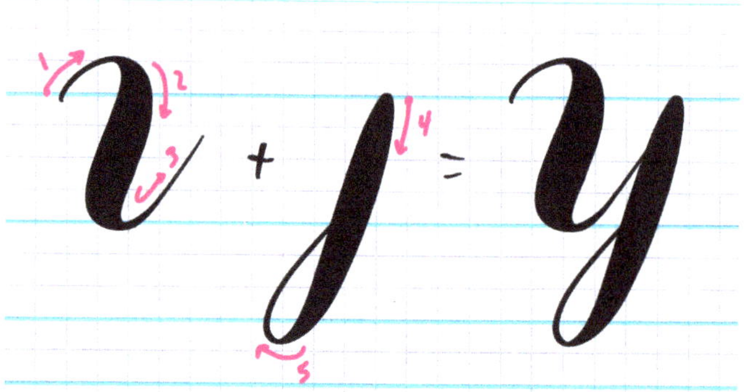

The lowercase "y" consists of an underturn and a descender loop. Note I've added that decorative little arch at the top of the underturn again. It's optional. You could start with a solid downstroke right from the waistline.

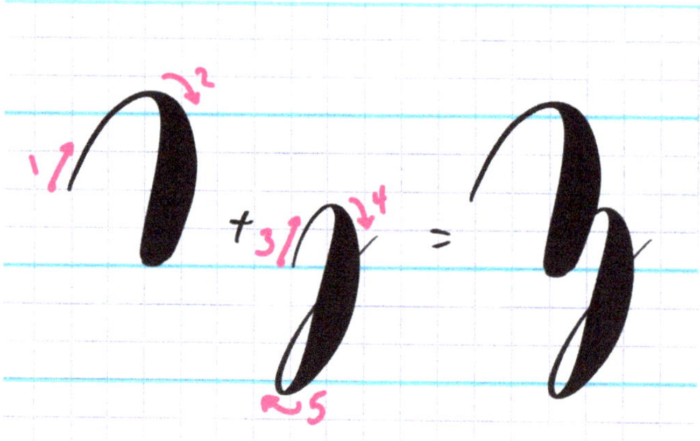

The lowercase "z" can look a bit tricky, but it is simply a partial overturn, followed by a mini overturn that transitions into a descender loop. Hey - wait a second - you've learned all the letterforms. Whoopa!

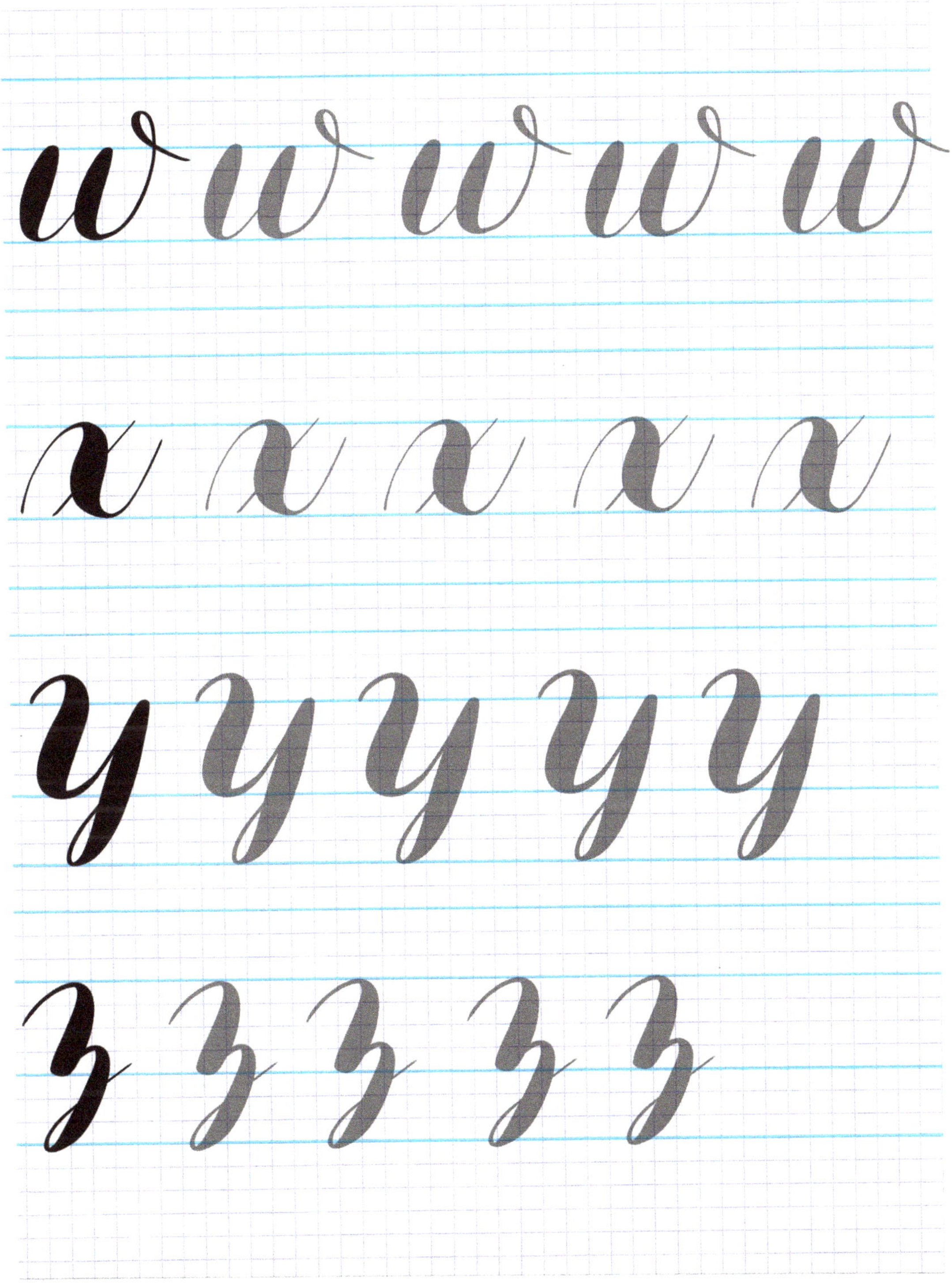

w w w w w

x x x x x

y y y y y

z z z z z

PRACTICE

minimum

zoom wow

happy

dogs rule

PAGES

coffee

hot cocoa

spooky

haunting

WAYS TO MAKE YOUR LETTERS POP

Try adding a drop shadow as with the word "groovy" below. This is done by using a grey or lighter hue than your main lettering and selecting a light source. In my example, I am suggesting the light comes from the top left and therefore casts a shadow on the right side of the letters. To achieve this, re-draw the letters with your lighter hue, keeping the drop shadow strokes down and to the right.

I added a few dots and dashes with a white gel pen for additional accents.

You can also use contrasting sizes of lettering and contrasting colours to make a statement as with the "hello winter" combination.

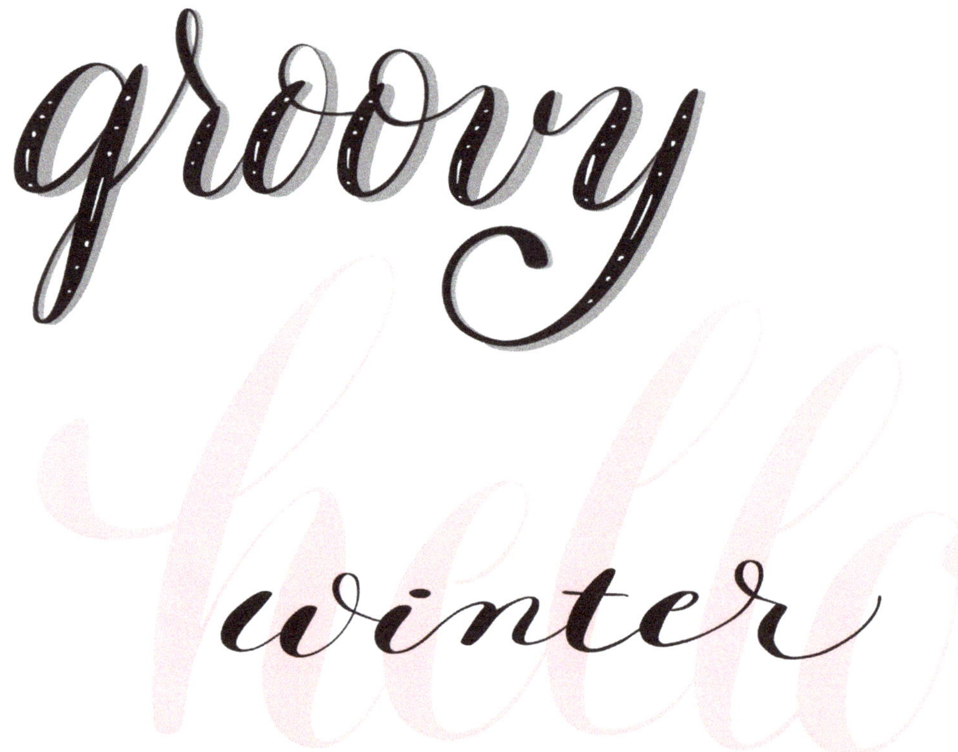

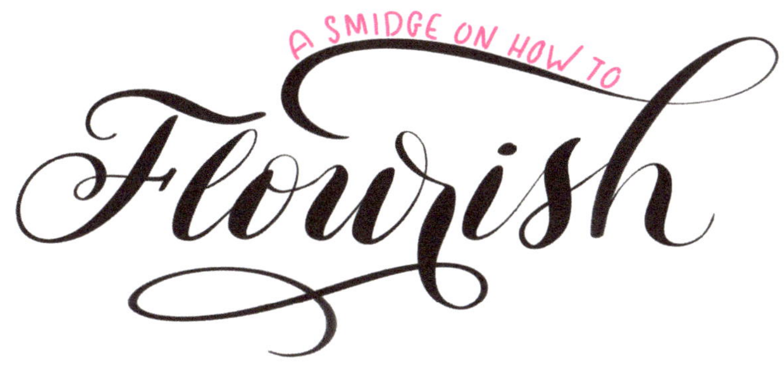

Flourishing is an advanced skill that I will touch on only briefly, but here are the nitty gritty basics. Great locations for flourishes are at the beginning or end of a word.

We know that how you form your ovals will effect the size and general shape of your letters. However, ovals are also a key component to beautiful flourishes.

A flourish starts with two ovals, side by side, as seen with the dotted pink examples in the image below. If you draw a line from the base of the first oval to the top of the second, you have created a smooth compound curve.

The combination of smooth compound curves, arching around those invisible ovals is the heart of flourishing. Experiment with how many different flourishes you can create just by sweeping your brush pen around the two ovals. Can you find hidden ovals (as shown in green dots in the image below) within lettering samples that you see on-line or in magazines?

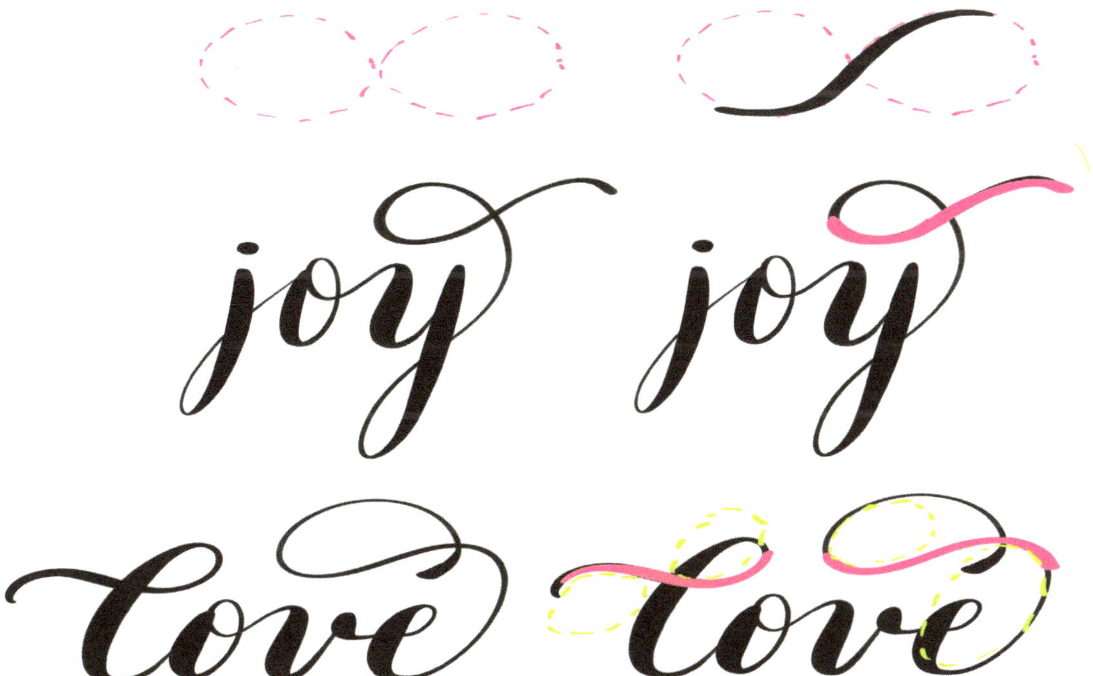

love

The word "love" to the left features a few alternate letter forms, specifically, an alternate "o" and an alternate "v" you might want to try. I've broken the strokes down for you in the images below. I've also provided several other alternates in case you're keen to experiment.

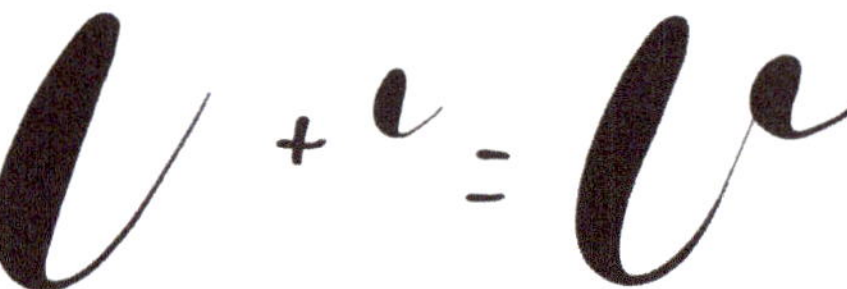

The example to the right demonstrates when to lift your brush pen and start the next letterform. The colour changes each time I lifted my pen from the paper. Lettering is not a flowing cursive style. It is a drawing of each letter individually, slowly, and with a lift of your brush after each stroke in the letterform.

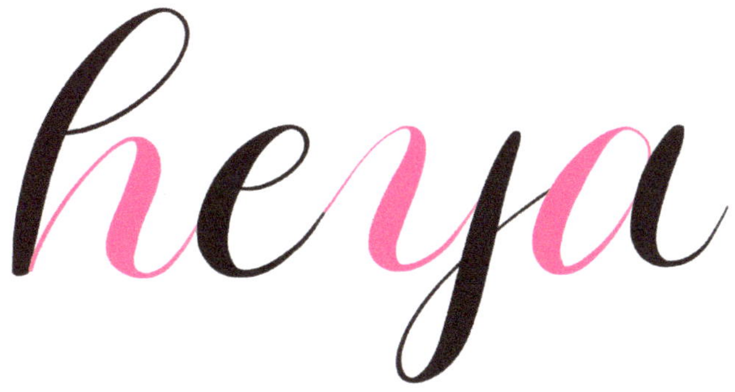

Once you have the basics down, you can adjust your lettering for different style, mood, and effects. Below are several examples that show just how much emotion and personality can be infused into each letter or word, simply by playing with the connections between letters, the slant, spacing, flourishes and swashes.

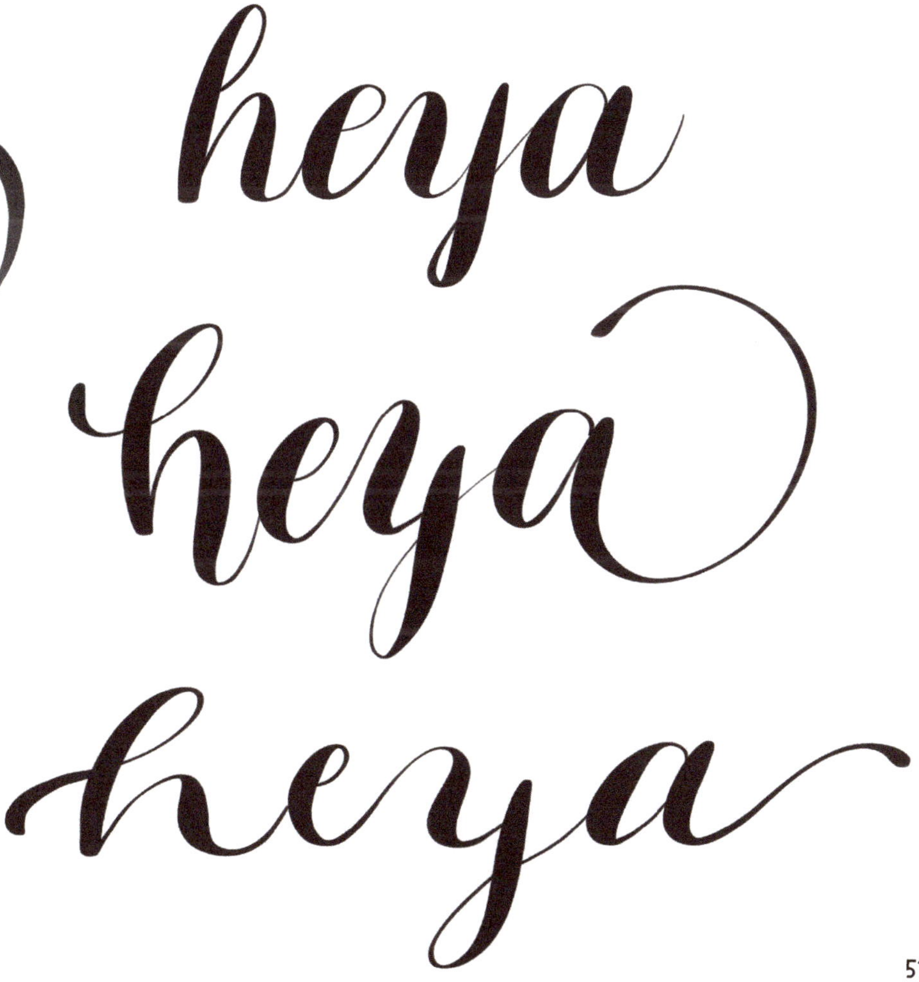

heya

heya

heya

Now that we've made it this far, there's something I have to tell you.

Ready?

Take a deep breath. This is important.

Going over the basic strokes and letterforms once or twice, or even ten times isn't going to be enough.

Just like me and my lettering crew below, you'll have to spend regular and consistent time on your lettering. The more time you spend practicing, the faster the forms will become muscle memory and the smoother and steadier your lettering will be.

I don't want this to stress you out. Practice is soothing for me. I set the stage a bit and have my favourite music playing, my dog sleeps at my feet, and the coffee is on. Take time out of your busy day to create and build your skills. You're worth every second.

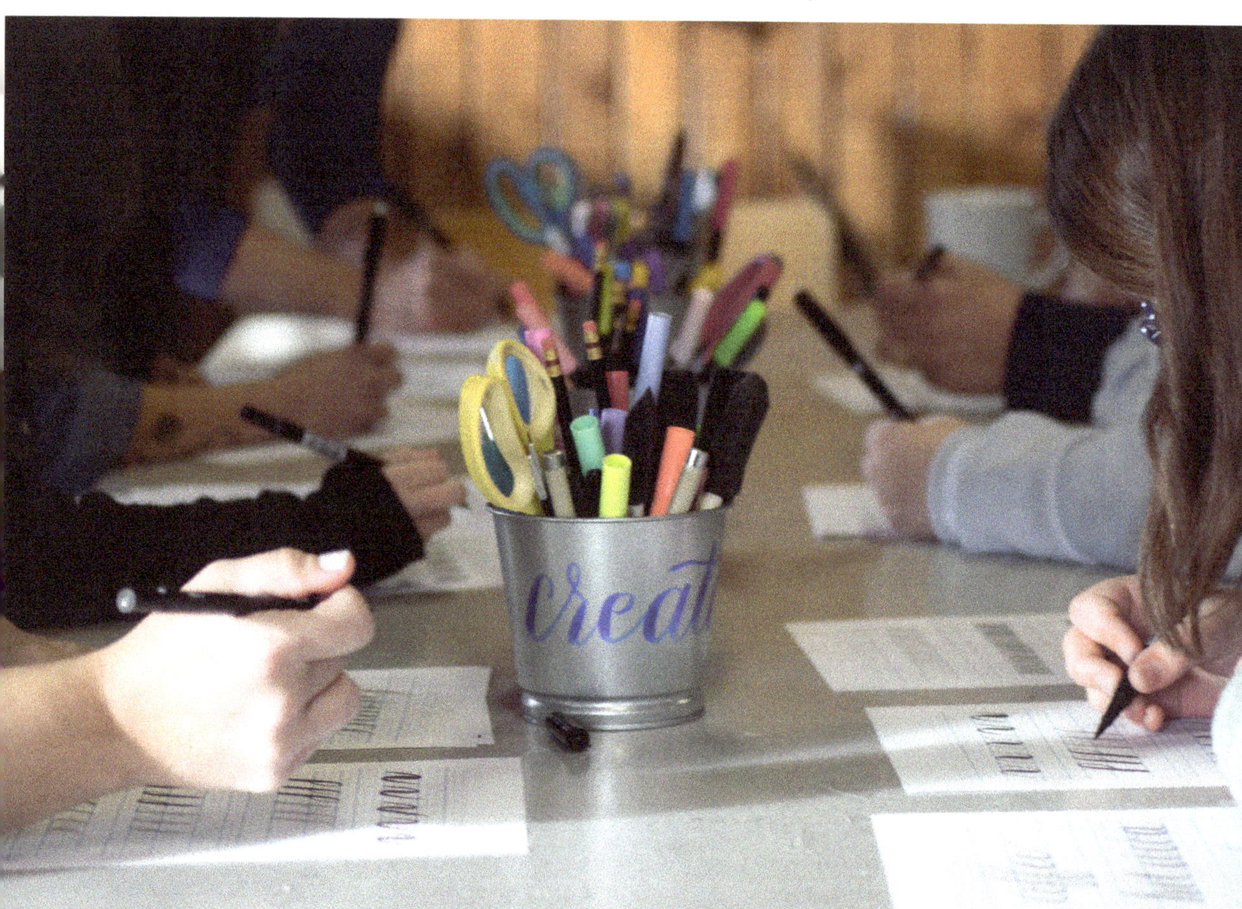

SAMPLE UPPERCASE

There are numerous ways to form uppercase letters and some are more ornate than others. Here is a basic style to get you started.

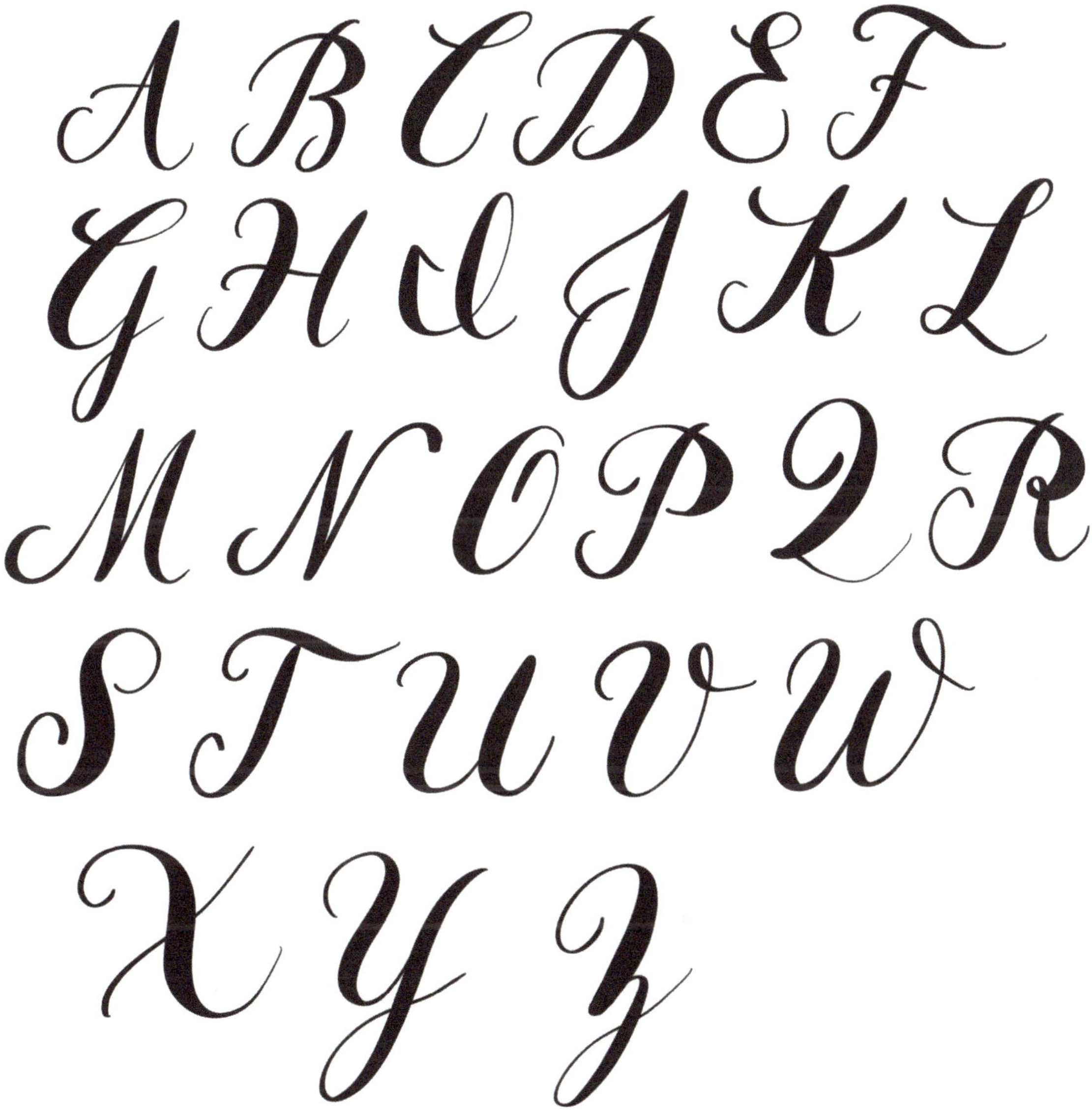

A B C D E F

G H I J K L

M N O P Q R

S T U V W

X Y Z

Below, I've indicated the order and direction of your strokes in order to create this style.

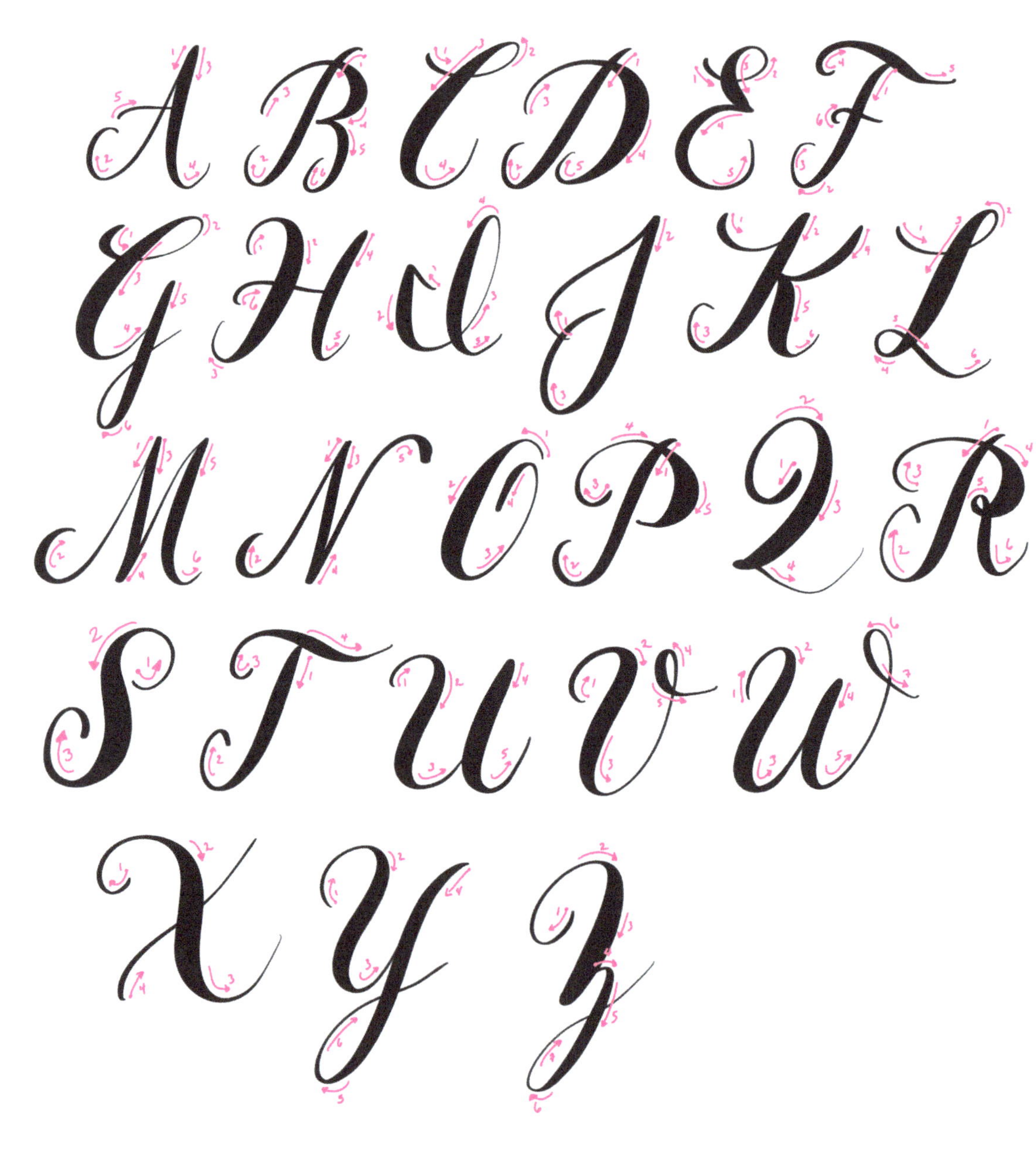

Here is a lighter sample for you to photocopy onto quality paper (as discussed on page 13) and then letter on directly.

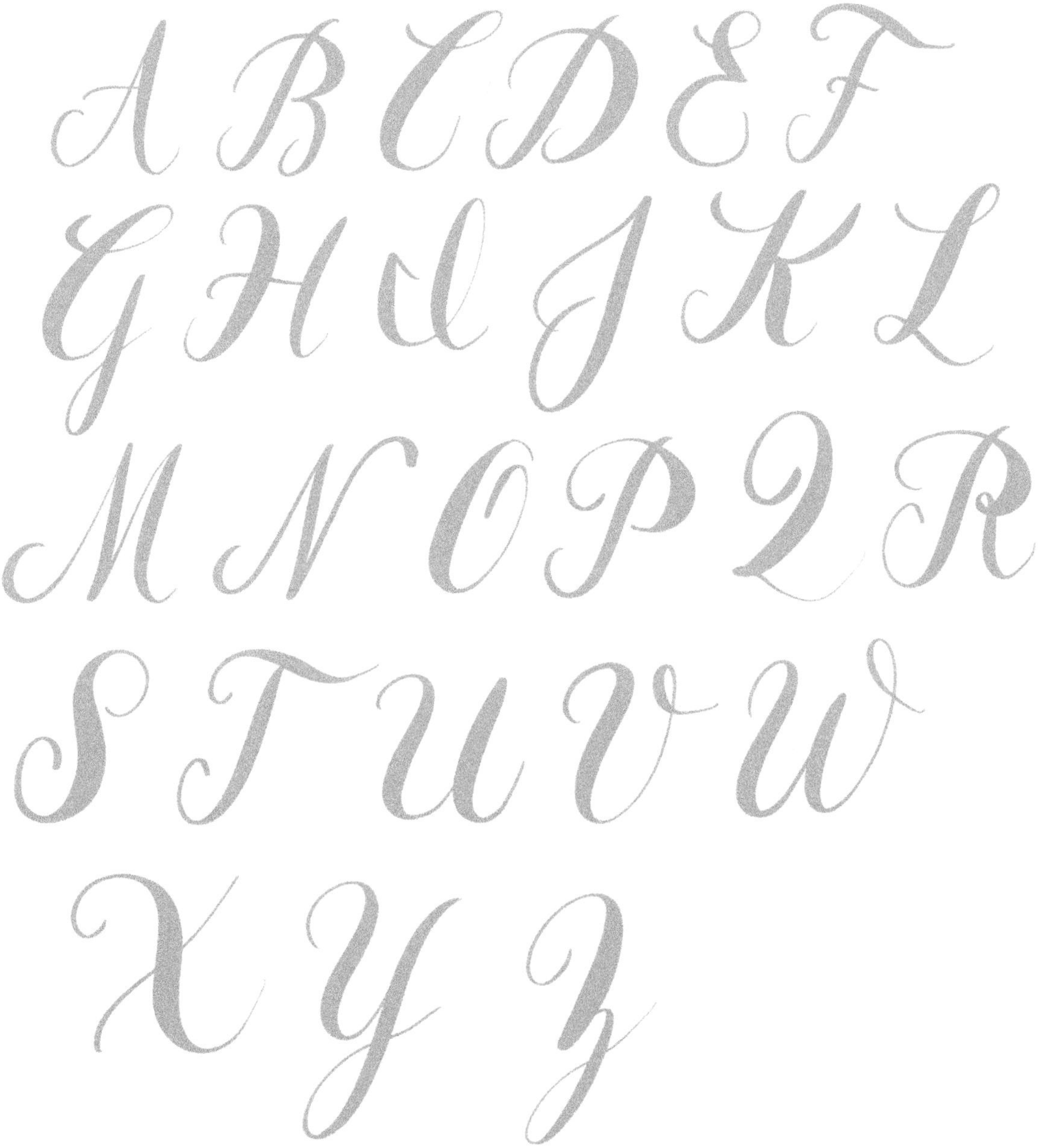

A B C D E F

G H I J K L

M N O P Q R

S T U V W

X Y Z

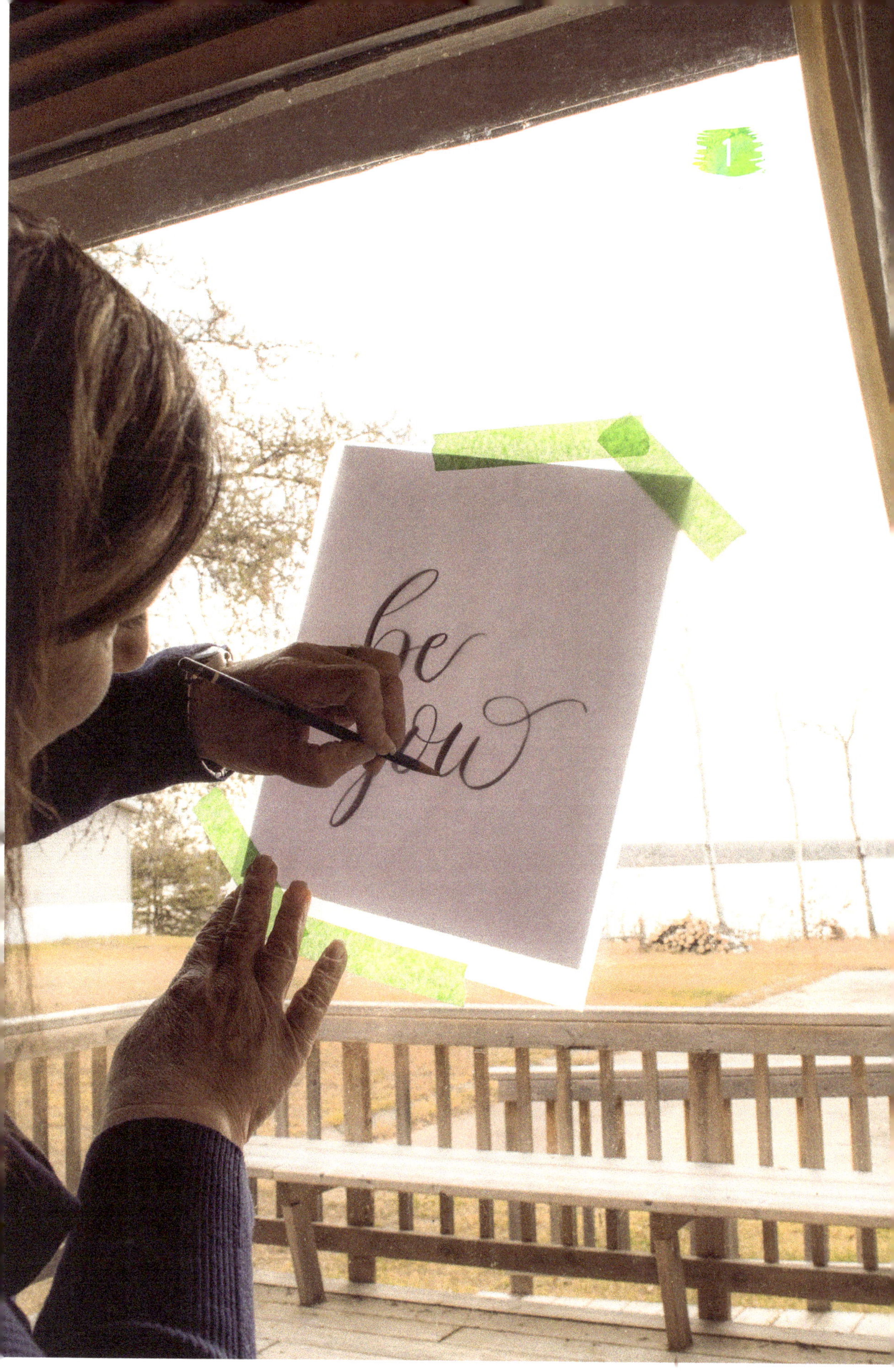
1
be you

TRANSFER TECHNIQUES

For several projects in this book, you'll need a way to transfer your lettering, or designs onto another surface, such as watercolour paper. Below are three methods you will find useful.

1. BRIGHT WINDOW

A very simple and cost effective way to transfer. With painter's tape, mount the image to be traced to a window with maximum sun exposure. Place another sheet of paper over top and you should be able to see a very distinct outline for tracing.

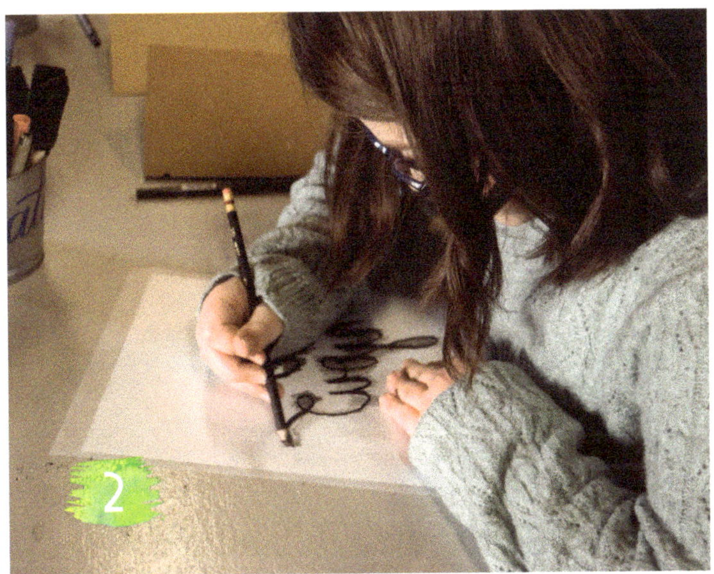

2. TRACING PAPER AND GRAPHITE

Flip your source image over and using an HB pencil or graphite pencil, shade over the lines. Place this sheet on top of your intended surface (graphite side down) and then redraw the original image. The shading you created will make an impression, enough for you to then clean up the lines as needed.

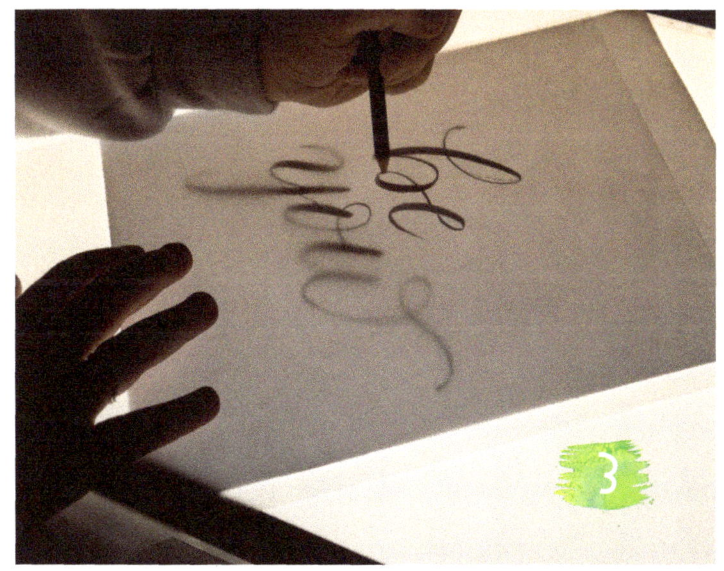

3. LIGHTPAD OR LIGHT BOX

Similar to bright window option, lightpads or light boxes provide a strong light source via a flat, tabletop surface.

the projects #1

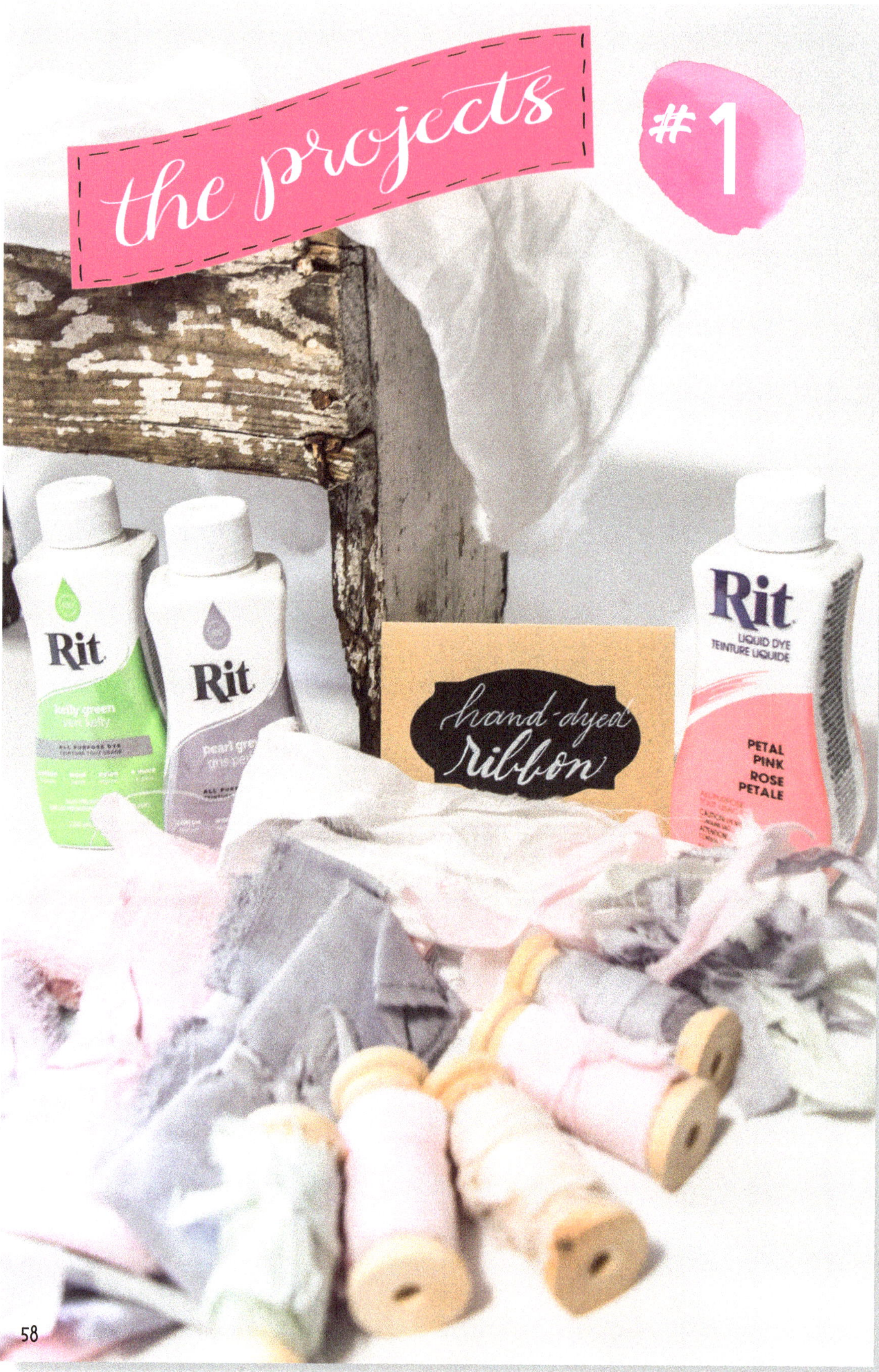

hand-dyed ribbon

DIY (DYE-IT-YOURSELF) RIBBON

I've placed this activity before the others as it's great to have some pre-made to use in subsequent projects. It's suprisingly easy (and fun!) to do.

If you're creating a large vat or batch of ribbon for a big project and need to recreate the same colour at a future date, I recommend taking detailed notes of your process.

Which fabric did you use? How wide did you cut and tear the strips? What was your exact dye to water ratio? How long did you leave the fabric sitting in the dye? Did you hang to dry inside your home or did the ribbon dry outside under direct sunlight? All of these factors can slightly alter the end result.

I enjoy a creative approach to ribbon dyeing and often vary the amount of time I leave swatches in the dye to have a range of hues. The longer the fabric sits in the dye, the deeper the colour, or I may leave different sections of the same ribbon in the dye for a longer time than others to create gradient or ombre effects.

Nature itself is unpredictable and perfectly imperfect, as are we all.

SUPPLIES

- Liquid Rit dye
- White linen fabric
- Scissors
- Large bowl
- Warm water
- Tongs or wooden spoon
- Wooden spools
- Area to hang dry (with perhaps a towel for drips)

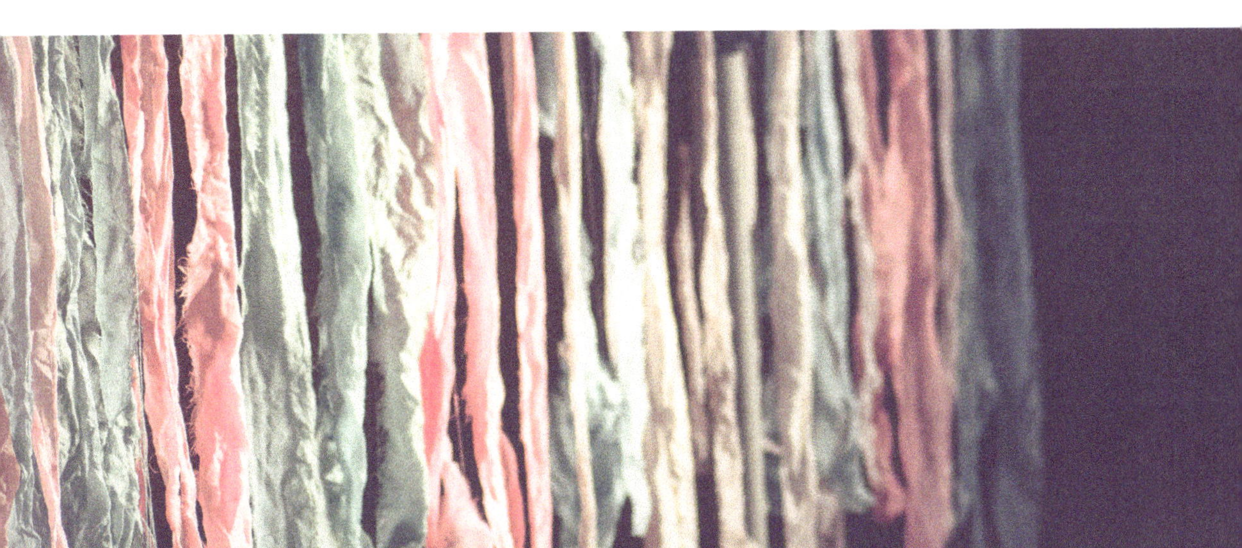

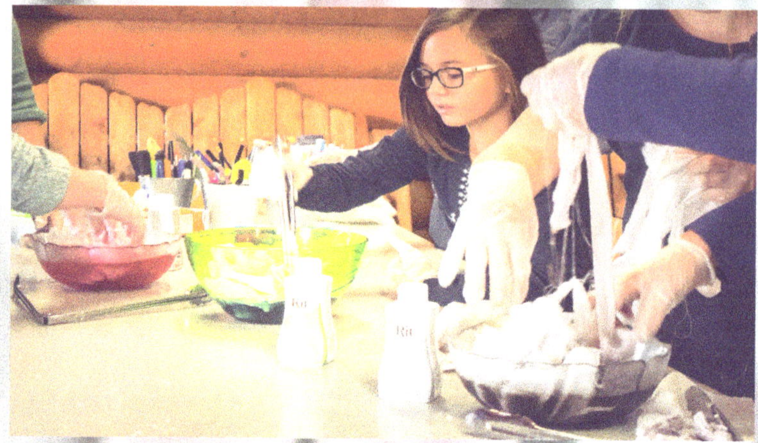

INSTRUCTIONS

Using sissors, and with the grain, cut small nicks at the edge of your fabric that are the intended width of your strips (ideally every 1 to 2 inches apart). Hand tear the strips by pulling the edges. The material will rip evenly along the thread grain.

Prepare RIT dye and water mixture as per the instructions on the packaging and in colours of your choice. You may want to use latex gloves to avoid dyeing your hands.

Place small bunches of strips in the dye mix and submerge them fully. Stir with metal tongs until the strips have taken on a hue you're happy with, but keep in mind they will dry lighter than they appear in the mixture. The longer you keep them in the dye, the deeper the hue. Anywhere from two to ten minutes should provide enough of a range in colours for you. These dyes work quickly, so any longer wouldn't be necessary. If the colour isn't as deep as you wanted, try again, but add more dye to the mix to concentrate the colour.

When you're ready wring the strips to remove as much liquid as possible and hang to dry. This may take from 20 to 30 minutes. If it's a sunny, warm day, hanging the strips outside is ideal. A drying rack with an extendible rod is handy if you have one.

TIPS

Hand-torn fabric will have stray threads. Once dry, you can trim off any extreme offenders, but the strays are part of the charm.

If you find your ribbon is too ragged or bumpy, you can iron it flat if necessary. I've used a regular iron and ironing board, as well as a hairstyling flat iron. Both methods work well, just be careful not to burn yourself. Young people will want help from adults for this.

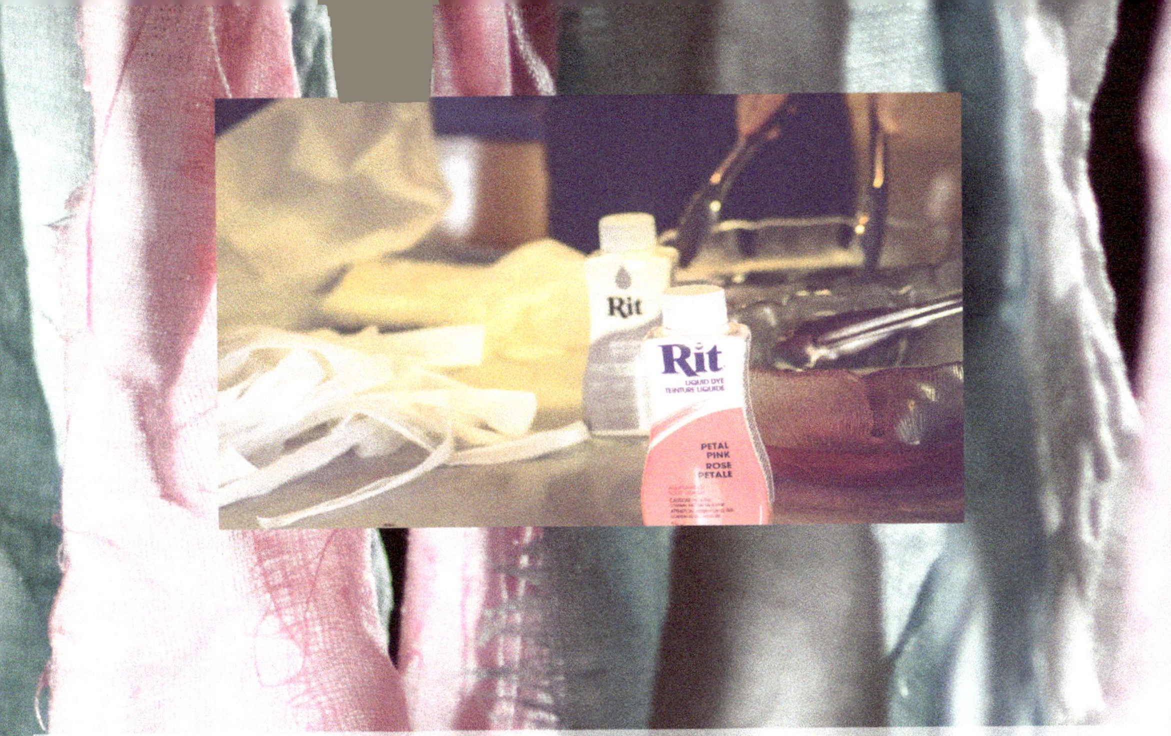

Once you've made a few yards of ribbon you'll have it on hand any time you want to up your elegance factor. It can be the finishing touch on chalk-painted mason jars (see the project on page 92), an embellishment to or replacement for gift wrapping, a delicate addition to flower arrangements, Easter baskets, wreaths, use it to create bracelets or necklaces, or tie it around greeting cards or invitations. When you need some instant charm – just add your own hand-dyed ribbon!

VARIATIONS

Raw fabric. Fabric not previously dyed by a manufacturer (usually a taupe tone) can be used instead of fabric already dyed white. Just note that it may be more difficult to obtain in a local fabric store.

Different fabrics. For a more informal projects, cotton works exceptionally well. And for a more luxurious feel, you can't get more fairy tale dreamy than silk.

Dye mixes. RIT dyes can be blended together to create unique colours.

Plant dyes. If you want a more organic method to avoid the use of chemical dyes, many leaves, berries, flowers, and spices produce an amazing array of hues and tones. This is a time consuming however, as you simmer a "soup" of your plant mixtures for up to several days to achieve the most vibrant colours.

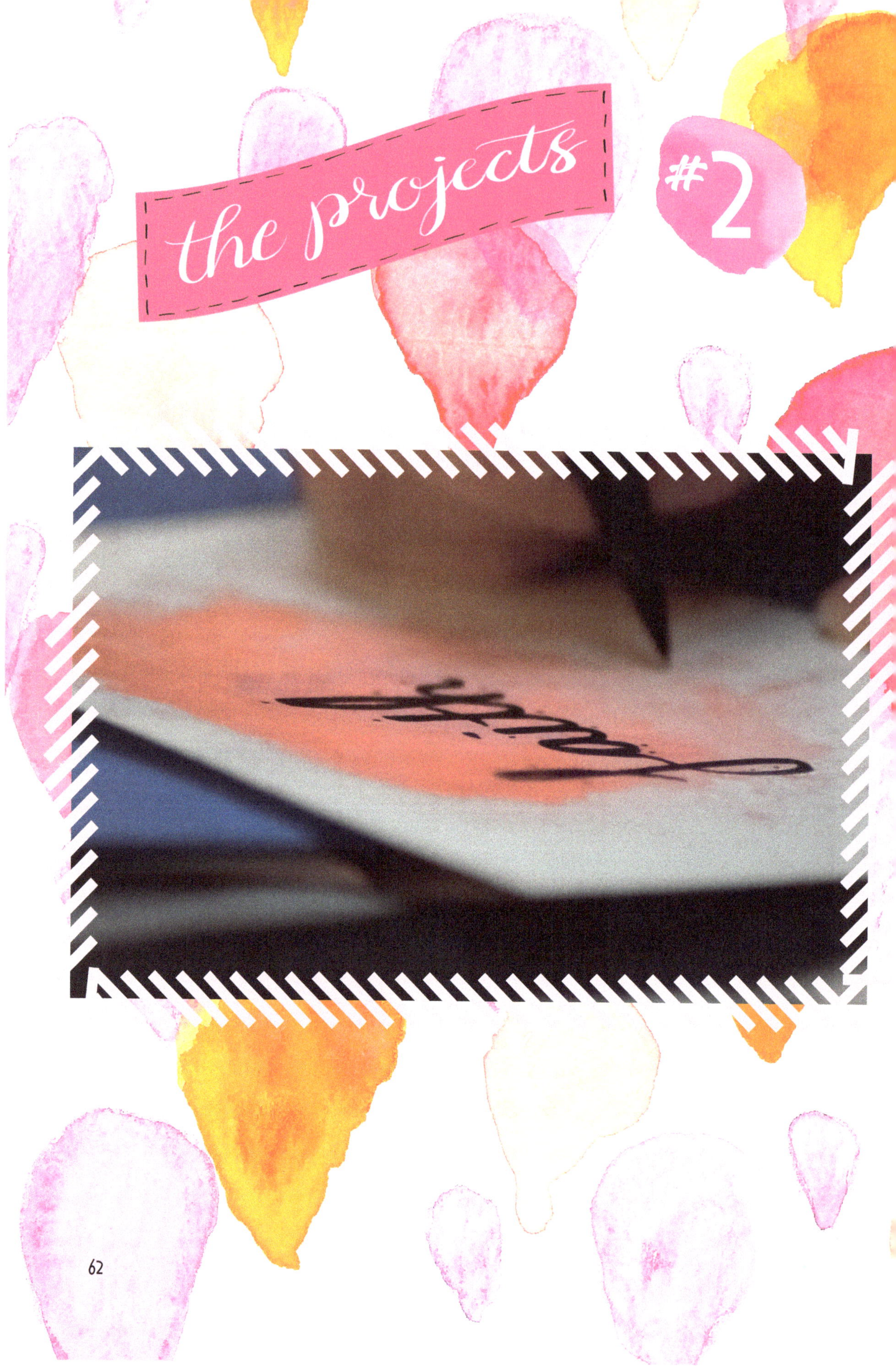
the projects
#2

WATERCOLOUR QUOTES

I'M A COLLECTOR OF
BEAUTIFUL THINGS.

They can be old or new, or new to me, and with writing and lettering, I collect words. Phrases. Quotes. Ones that resonate with me at that moment, and once discovered, are jotted down in my coil notebook for safe keeping.

Later, I'll flip through that notebook and choose to letter one of my treasures and perhaps add a bit of watercolour or an illustration to enhance the meaning or hint at an emotion I'd like to share.

There are instances where I create a watercolour background for a specific piece of lettering. This is when I already have an idea of the colour, texture, or pattern I'd like to feature and sit down to create a single work just for that purpose.

But often I'm able to skim through various backgrounds I've already created to see what will work with the lettering. You can have a lot of fun and be quite creative if you set aside some time just to create a variety of backgrounds for later use.

INSTRUCTIONS

SUPPLIES

- Watercolours
- Watercolour paper (cut to 5x7 or post-card size)
- Paint brush
- Container of water
- Papertowel
- Black brush pen

BACKGROUNDS

Dip your brush into clean water and paint the water onto your canvas in a random manner. Be careful here; too much water will warp the paper, and too little won't allow the colours you're going to add bleed or flow together. Once you have a nice sheen of water in a pleasing shape on your paper, load your brush with a colour and drop it onto your canvas. Allow the colour to spread. If it isn't spreading, add more water to your brush and re-drop in the same spot, prompting the colour to flow. Be sure to leave white space to act as highlights and to allow room for more colours.

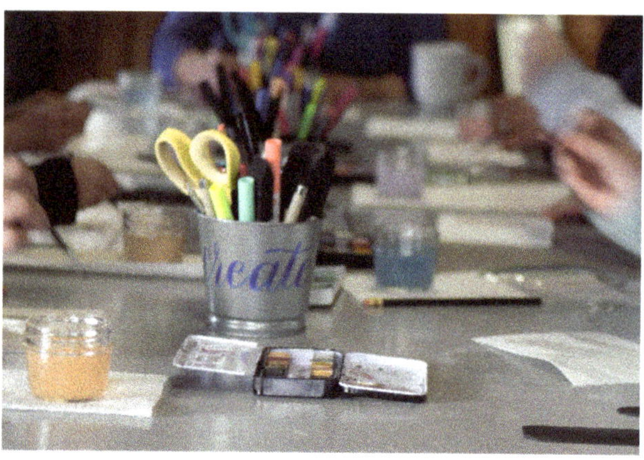

Clean your brush and load it with a complementary colour. Drop it onto your canvas in new locations, but also near or directly overlapping the original colour. Add another colour if you'd like, but remember, too many and you run the risk of overcooking your background. It's possible to create beautiful backgrounds with even a single colour. The wonder of watercolour is that by adding more water, or more paint, you change the opacity and hue of a single colour so that it can provide numerous shades. For the best results, I suggest sticking with 1-3 colours to start and experiment with adding more once you've dabbled a bit with the possibilities watercolours can offer. The goal is to allow the colours to blend and flow together in places, remain all their own in others, and yet still have those whitespaces for glimmers of light.

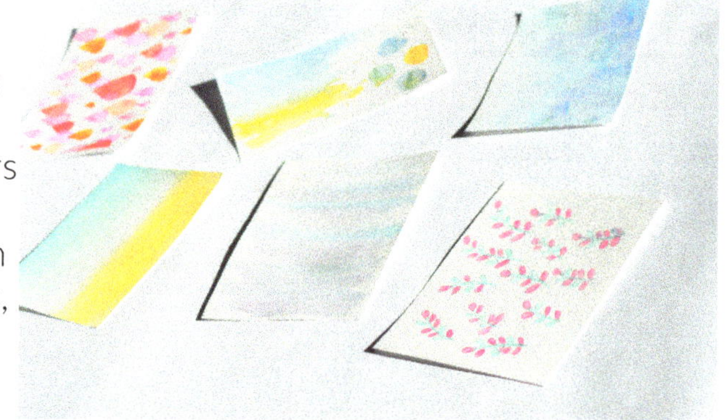

Set this canvas aside and follow the same steps to complete the rest of the canvases you've precut.

Experimenting is key here. Aim to make each canvas unique, unless you're creating similar backgrounds for multiple copies of the same project (place cards for a dinner party), or for a series of projects (eg: a bunch of red backgrounds with different Christmas phrases). Allow plenty of time for your canvases to dry. Keep them in an album or folder as a stash of ready-made backgrounds to choose from at a later date. And/or scan them to create digital versions.

LETTERING

Grab some scratch paper and a pencil and create several thumbnail sketches to plan the layout of your text. Single words are usually centered on the canvas, but can still be sketched in a variety of lettering styles and sizes, and you may want to add a related illustration to enhance the meaning. Planning these elements out in thumbnails allows you to see the overall shape and flow of your composition. This way you can choose the best bits of each sketch and compile them into one amazing final draft to transfer to your watercolour background.

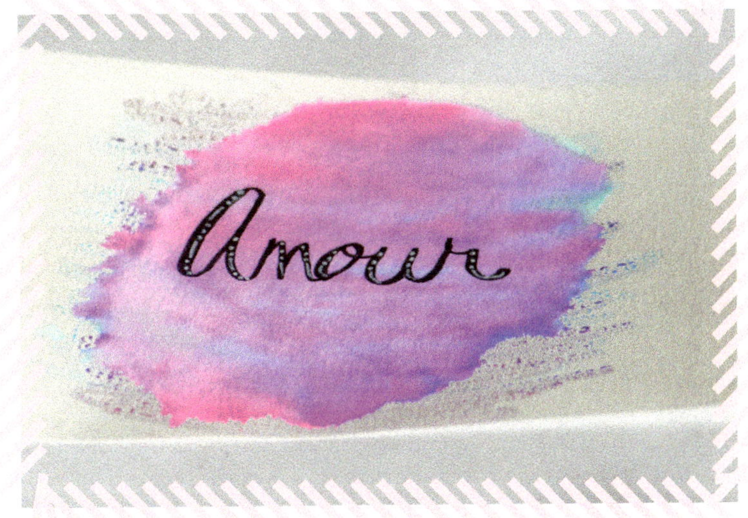

Take your time with this design stage. Phrases or quotes can be broken down into individual elements and lettering styles for the most impact. By pre-planning, just as how I plot and outline before I begin to write my fiction work, will result in a much more cohesive and appealing final product.

Use one of the three transfer techniques discussed on page 56. Trace your design with the lettering tool and method of your choice - black Tombow, a waterbrush pen loaded with a vibrant and contrasting colour. Add gel pen or drop shadows or other embellishments to the design as desired.

VARIATIONS

- Experiment with dots, dashes, squiggles, straight and curved lines, shapes, textures and test colour combinations.
- Cut a few of your 5x7 pieces in half and see what you come up with when you're forced to work on a smaller canvas. These can be used for backgrounds of single words for envelope confetti.

WATERCOLOUR GIFT TAGS

There are so many ways to use watercolour with lettering. Place cards at weddings or special events, greeting cards, and of course, gift tags.

INSTRUCTIONS

On a piece of cardstock paper, trace the gift tag shapes from the templates on page 116 and cut them out.

Use the cut out shapes as outlines for your gift tags. Trace as many as you can onto your watercolour paper, turning and angling them as needed. Be sure to leave a bit of a gap between the outlines for easy cutting later, and also in case your watercolour strays outside the lines.

SUPPLIES

- Watercolours
- Watercolour paper
- Paint brush
- Container of water
- Papertowel
- Black brush pen

In this example we created Christmas gift tags and selected red and green paints, but you can choose any colour that matches your theme or preference.

Paint your tags with your theme in mind. Small egg shapes or water drops for spring themes, flowers for summer or anniversaries, pumpkins for fall, or random patterns and blends that will suit any occasion. Plaids and stripes work well for Christmas, as shown here.

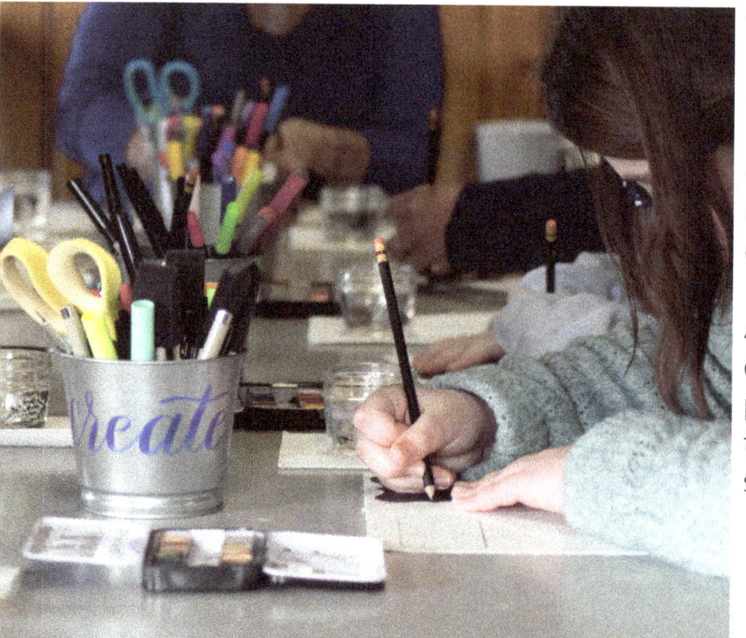

Let dry.

Carefully cut out your tag. Punch a hole in a logical location; usually centered and close to the edge.

Add a length of your own hand-dyed ribbon (see instructions on page 58), store-bought ribbon, twine, raffia, or other kinds of string to act as a tie for your tag.

the projects #3

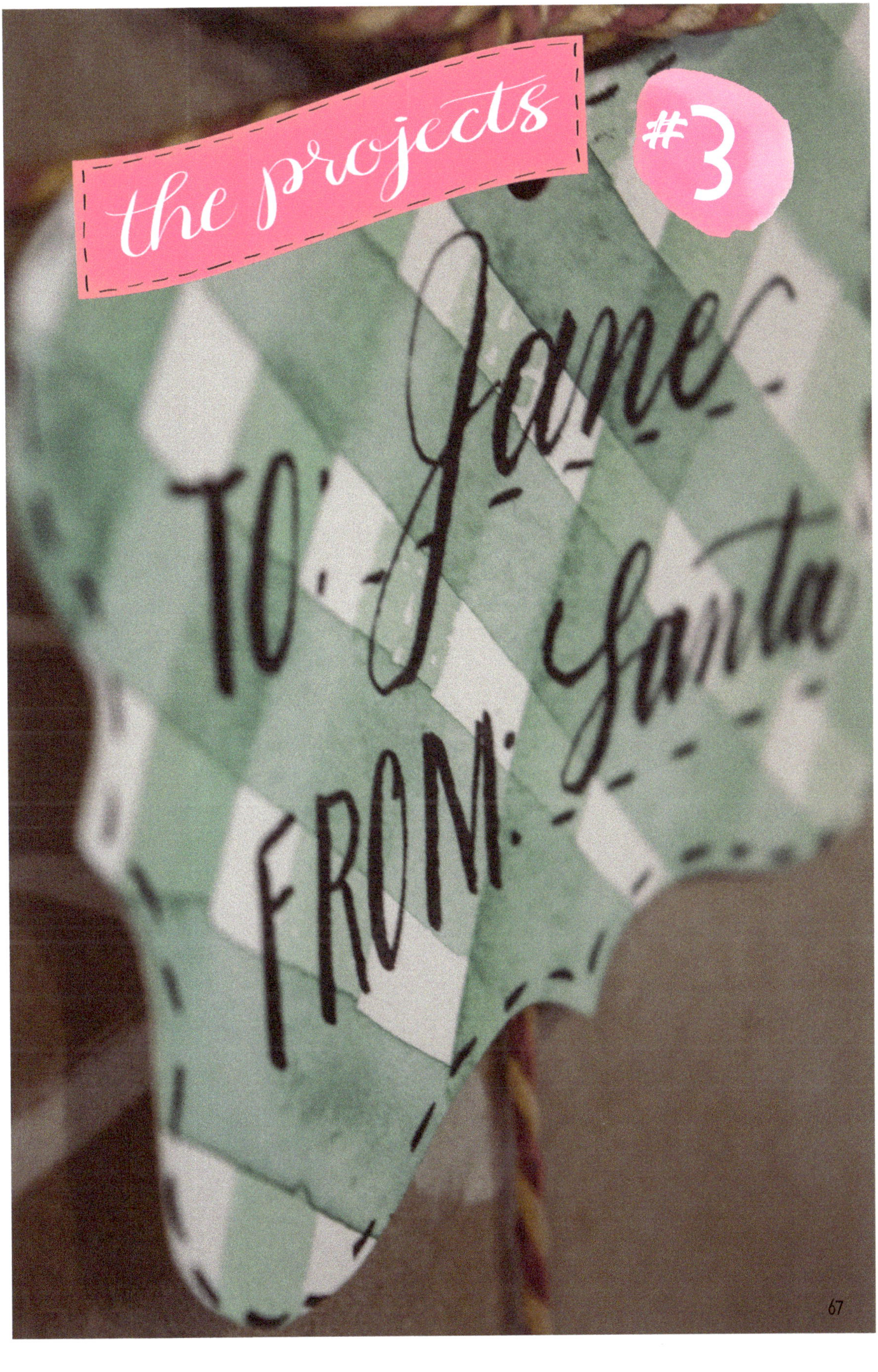

TO: Jane
FROM: Santa

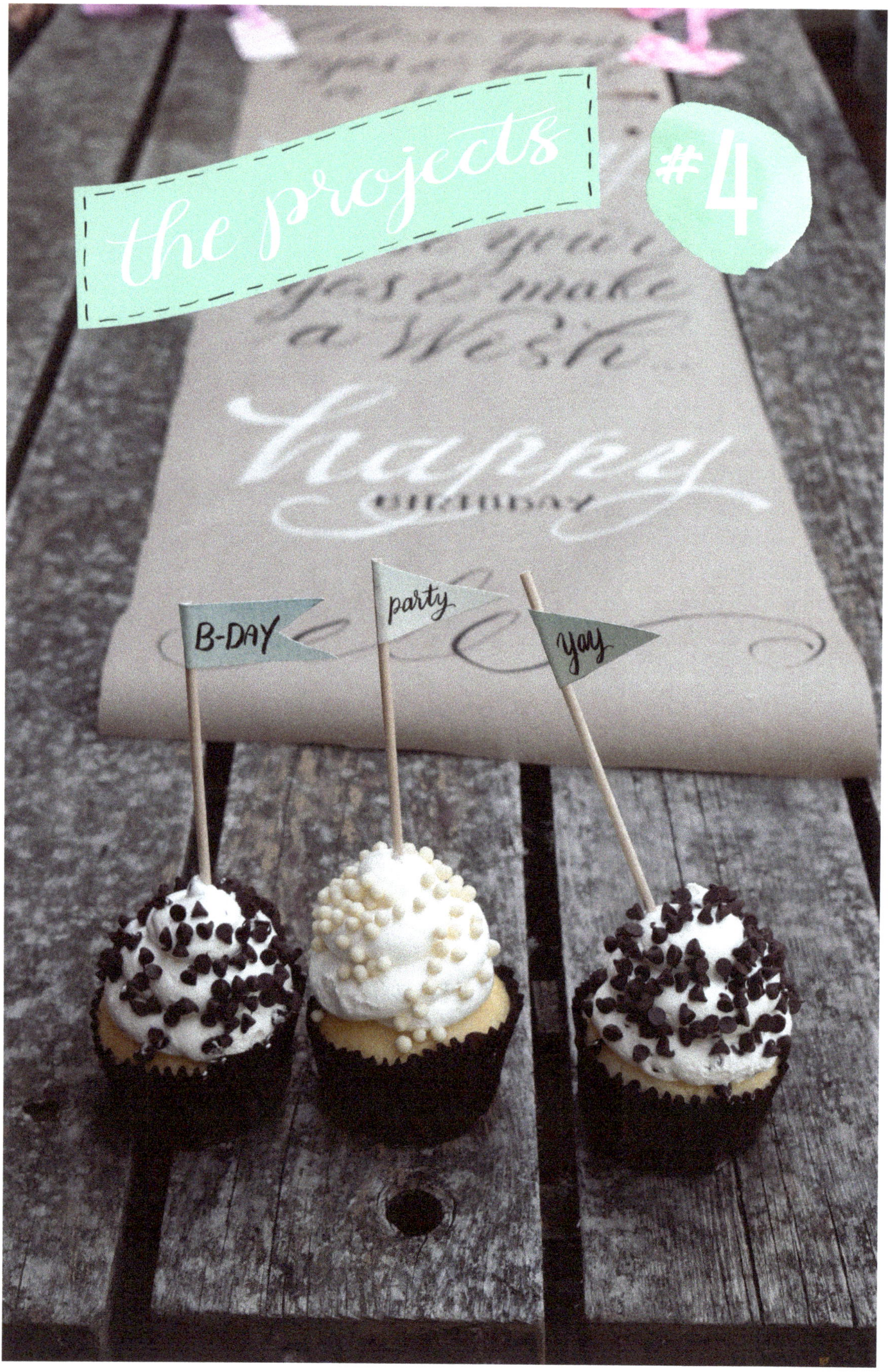

the projects #4

CUPCAKE TOPPERS

Consider the cupcake topper to be the exclamation point on a spectacularly delicious sentence. A feast for the eyes in more ways than one. Your toppers could be theme related puns, best wishes, or a few catchy words to capture the spirit of your event.

SUPPLIES

- Wood craft dowels
- Scissors
- Mod Podge sealant
- Scraps of watercolour practice paper
- Small tip black brush pen

INSTRUCTIONS

Trace the templates from page 115 onto a piece of cardstock, scrapbook paper, a watercolour background you've created (see instructions on page 62), watercolour paper with some colour tests or a piece you aren't planning on keeping, or any fairly firm paper that has a pleasing colour or pattern to serve as the background to your lettering.

Letter short words or phrases onto the shapes as space allows. Use a pencil to lightly add a guideline, or if you have a laser level handy, those work well and you don't have any lines to erase.

Lightly pencil in your lettering and tweak as needed. Once you're happy with your lettering, trace with lettering marker of your choice. Erase any pencil lines and cut out the completed shapes.

Wrap the cut shapes around the wood, craft dowel, leaving a bit of the dowel exposed at the top. When you're happy with the placement, fix in place with Mod Podge, white glue, or double sided tape. If gluing, hold in place and apply pressure for a few minutes for the paper to adhere to the dowel. Let dry.

Insert into cupcakes at the same angle and height for a more formal feel, or in random, quirky angles and various heights so each presentation is unique.

As you can see from the photo, these toppers go well with the kraft table table runner project coming up next.

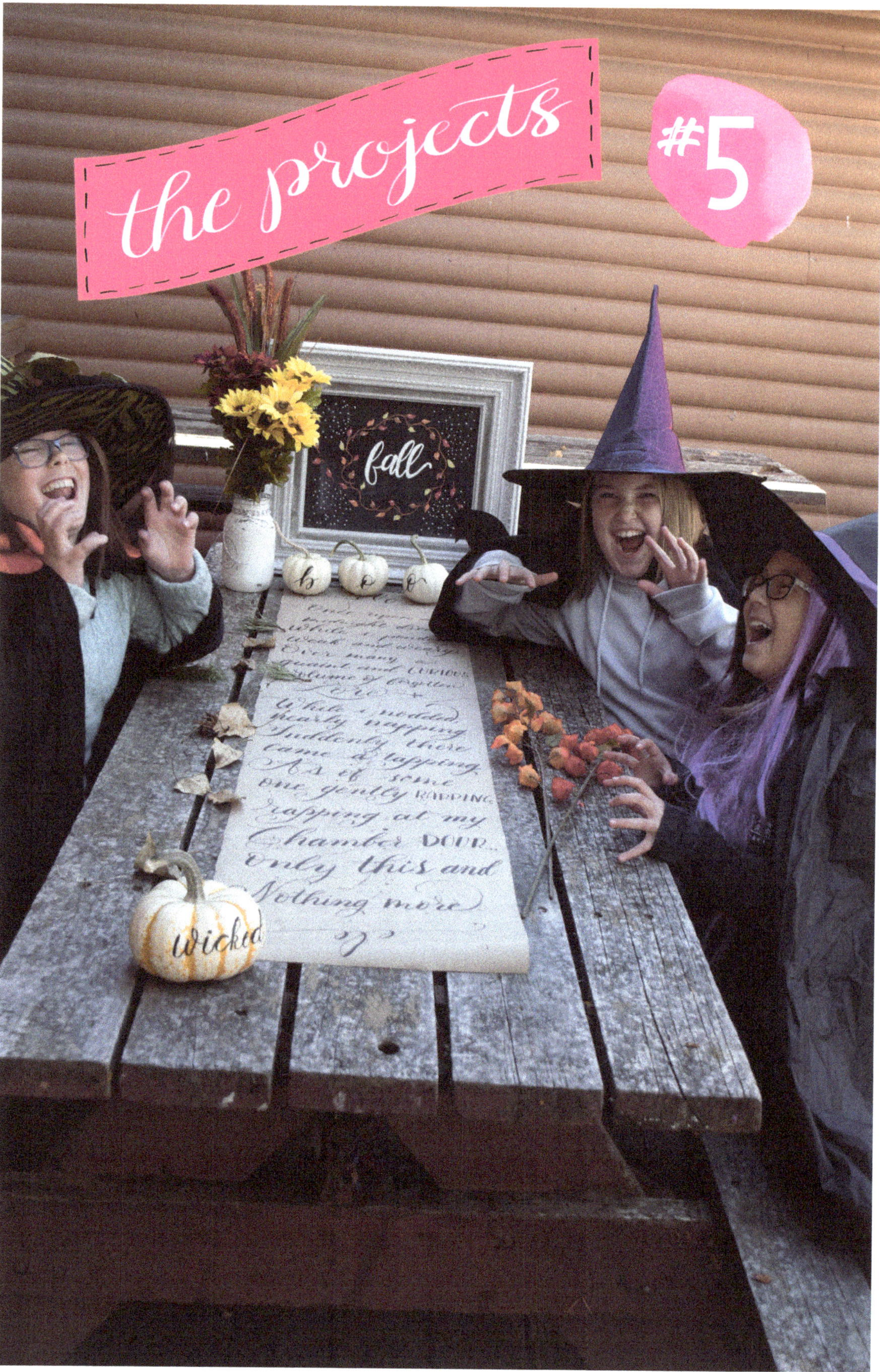
the projects
#5
fall
While I nodded
nearly napping
Suddenly there
came a tapping
As if some
one gently RAPPING
rapping at my
Chamber DOOR..
Only this and
Nothing more
wicked

KRAFT PAPER TABLE RUNNER

Kraft paper is a natural fit for brush lettering as the surface is smooth, it's environmentally friendly, and inks take on a rustic look with this warm-toned background. A hand-lettered table runner is a unique way to accent any table setting.

SUPPLIES

- Utility knife
- Measuring tape
- Ruler or laser level
- Pencil and eraser
- Brush pens in black, red, gold, silver
- Water-based white marker with a wide / extra bold tip
- Roll of heavy duty kraft paper wrapping paper (30 inches wide by 10 feet)
- Phrase or quotation to letter

INSTRUCTIONS

With a utility knife, cut a roll of kraft paper roll in half, creating two 15 inch wide rolls. One of these can serve as a back up if you need a do-over.

Measure the length of the table, which your runner will be placed upon. It's your choice here if you'd like to use the full roll and have room for the runner to drape down the ends of your table or if you wish to trim to a specific size. Trim as needed.

The key to this table runner is to write with fairly large lettering so the quote or phrase is visual from a distance and will still be seen when the table is set. If your lettering is too small, it won't have as much impact and the runner will take a substantial amount of time to complete.

Think large lettering, airy and sweeping across the page.

For best results, do a rough sketch or thumbnail of how the lettering might flow on the runner. This will also give you an idea of just how much of the actual quote you'll be able to fit on the runner. For a longer quote, decrease the size of your lettering or find a good spot to end the quote early. Then have it trail off with an ellipse and a fancy flourish or embellishment.

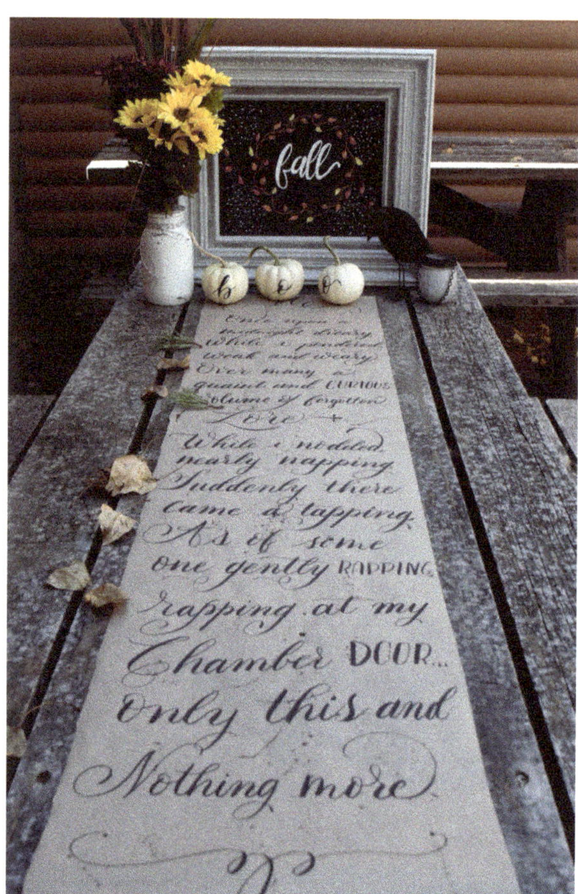

Using either a ruler or a laser level for guidelines and a pencil, lightly letter the quote on the runner. You may choose to work on a long table to see the runner as a whole, or work "scroll style", unrolling a section at a time as you work through the quote. Erase and fix any placement issues as required.

Letter over your pencil work with a tool of your choice. In these examples I used a combination of brush pens, some with metallic inks, and also an extra wide tip for the blocky, white text of "Happy Birthday". Erase any remaining pencil lines.

Shorter phrases can also be selected for this project. Just repeat it several times – either the same way, but divided with some blank space or a swash or flourish; or, letter with slight variations for added visual interest.

VARIATIONS

Create a Christmas, Halloween, or birthday themed table runner using metallic markers or adding glitter with gel pens or add a bit of ink spatter for drama.

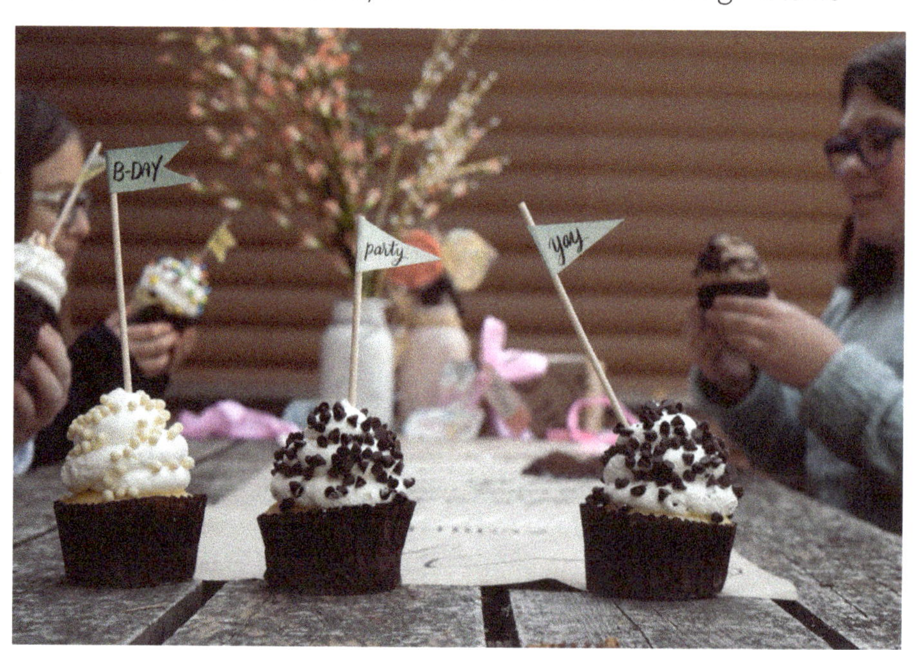

Choose any theme, quote, or holiday you desire as this project can be made to suit all events or celebrations.

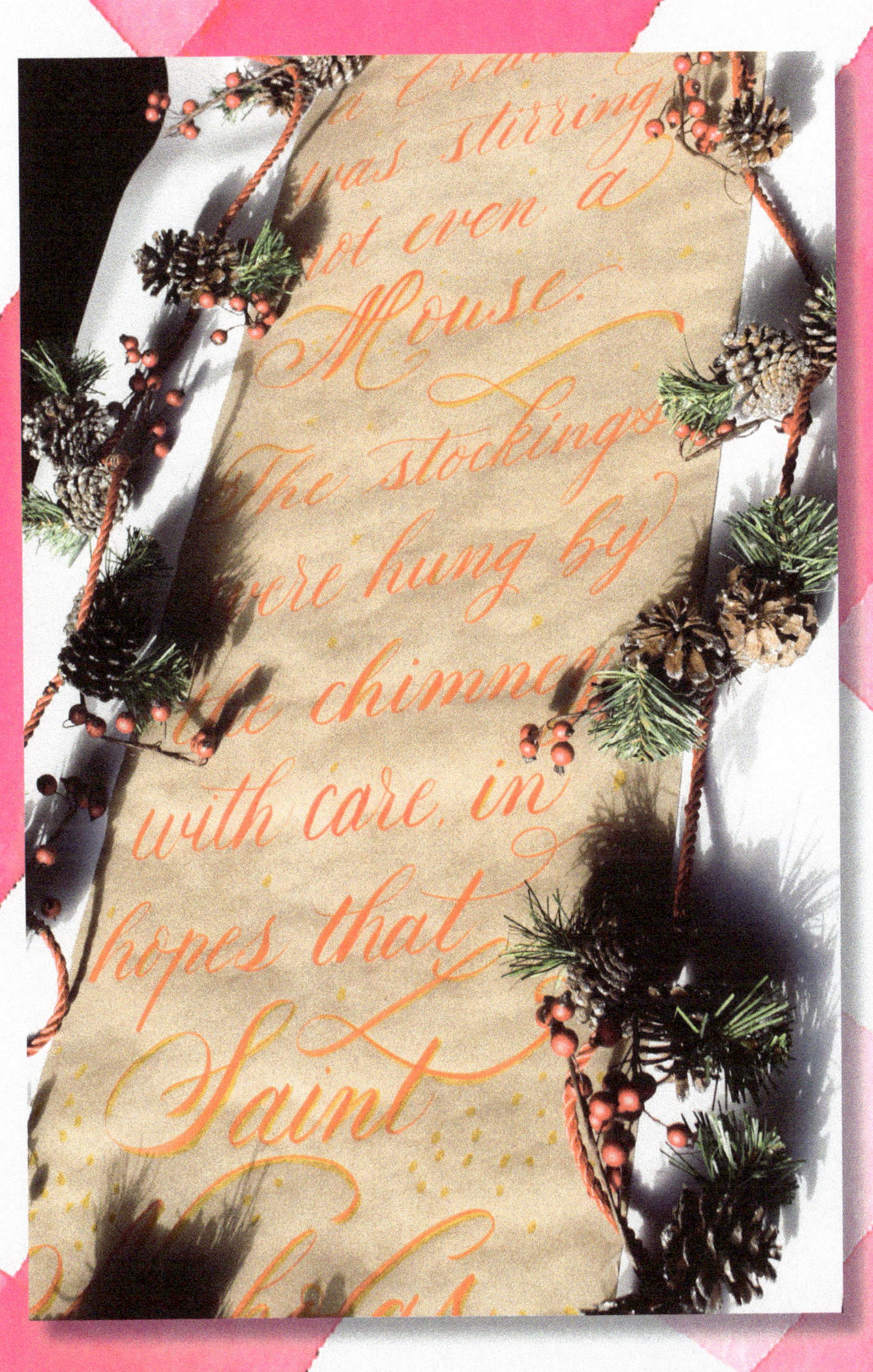
was stirring
Mouse.
The stockings
hung by
with care, in
hopes that
Saint

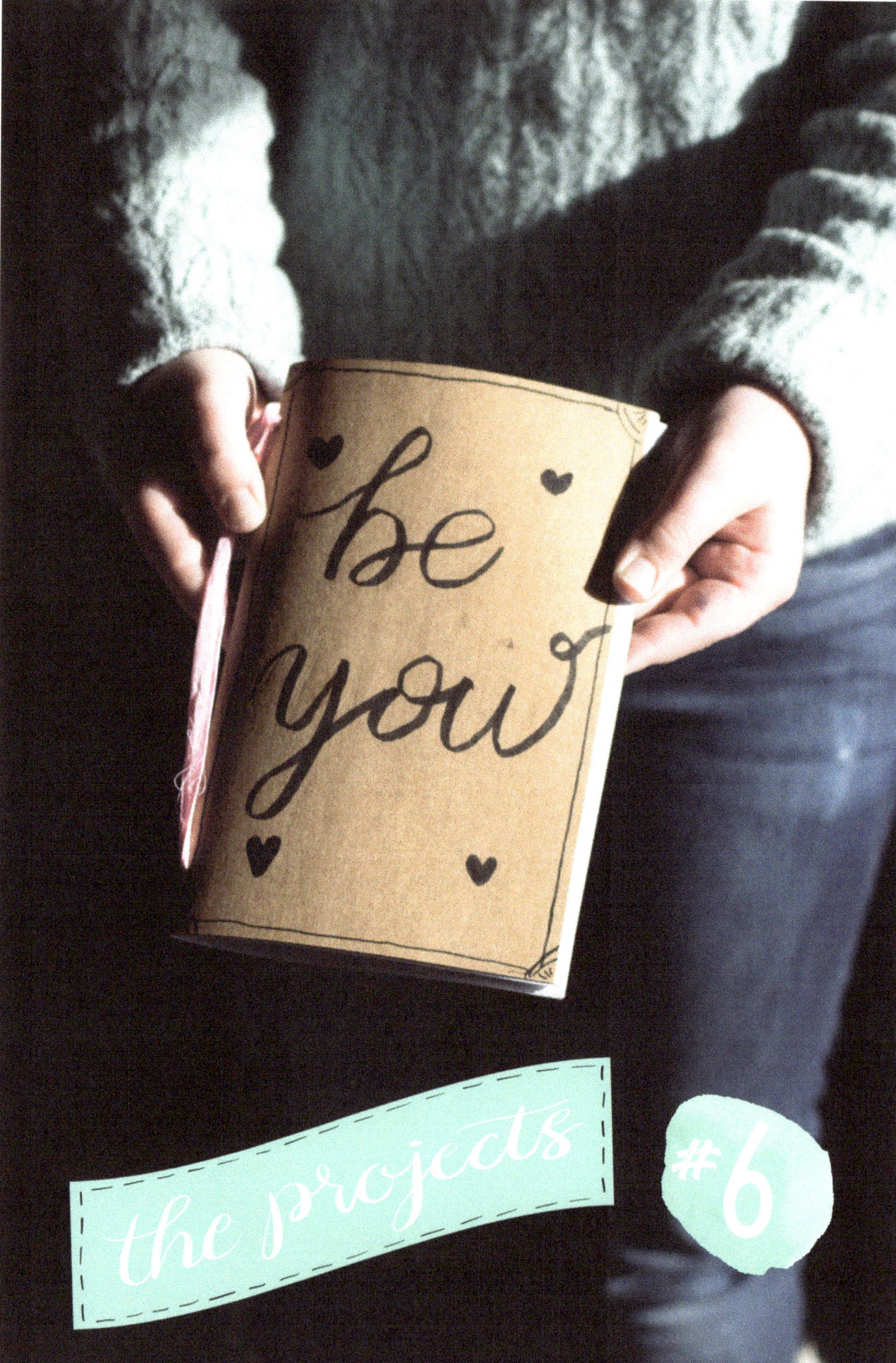
be you
the projects
#6

INSPIRATION JOURNALS

Diaries have been around for centuries and have retained specific features.

Entries are made in chronological order and individually marked with the date of writing. Entries are handwritten. Journals are more informal versions of diaries, without the need for daily entries. Diary, journal, notebook...these terms are used interchangeably. Whatever you call them, they document everything from the day-to-day grind, to our innermost thoughts and feelings, acting as snapshots of time periods and notable events.

Published diaries, such as the Diary of Anne Frank, give us valuable (and sometimes raw) first hand accounts and insights otherwise lost or omitted from other public records.

With the advent of the Internet, we've seen the trend of online diaries in the form of blogs and vlogs. When you think about it, social media sites like Facebook, Instagram, Twitter are one collective diary, documenting the daily lives, beliefs, loves, hates, lies, and truths of people across the globe.

We may be sharing more than ever before, but social media is often an arena of illusion. Posts are polished, photos are staged and edited for the most impact – this is the land of what we want people to see and may not always reflect our authentic selves.

This is where the resurgence of hand-written, personal diaries and journals comes in – these are written just for ourselves. They can have specific themes, such as sleep or dream journals, diet or healthy living journals, travel journals...or a single journal can contain elements of all these, and more. For example, there are numerous web-sites, blogs, and guidebooks outlining the current Bullet or dot journaling trend, that I, personally, want to dive into one of these days.

Here we're taking a simple and sweet approach to journaling. This project will encourage you, or some-one you care about, to take a few moments here and there to take up your pen and spend some time recording your thoughts, hopes, fears, dreams, or aspirations. I suggest inspirational phrases for the headers on these notebooks, such as: Be you, You got this, Choose joy, etc...but the message you select to letter on the cover can be heartfelt, funny and snarky, an inside joke, a seasonal greeting – it's up to you. That's the crazy beauty of a hand-made journal.

SUPPLIES

- 1 sheet of Kraft pa-per
- 10 sheets of blank or lined printer paper
- Scratch paper
- Whole punch
- Hand-dyed ribbon (see instructions page ___)
- Black brush pen

INSTRUCTIONS

Fold kraft paper in half and apply pressure to crease, this is the cover for our notebook Take note of the available room on the front cover and, using scratch paper, create thumbnail sketches of the cover design. This includes your main lettering and any other illustrations you wish to include.

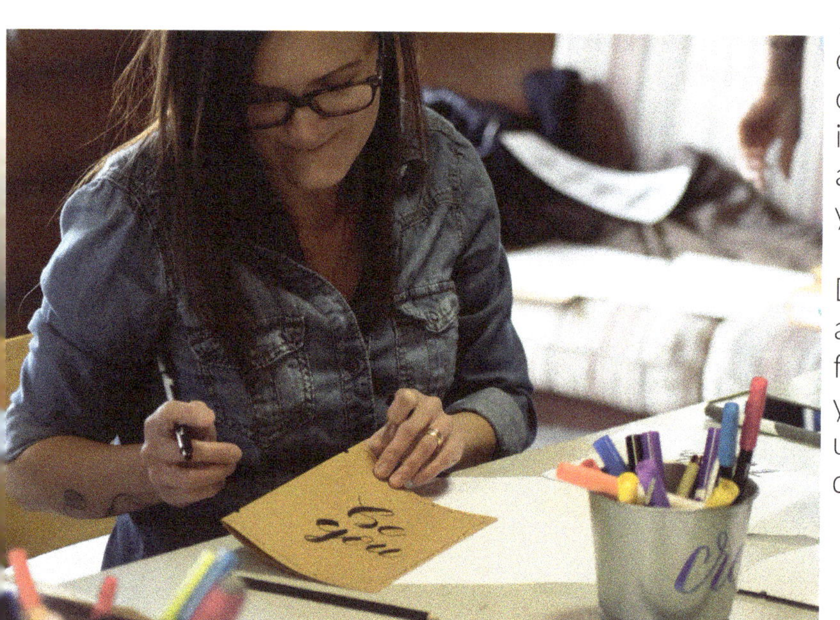

Decide on the best version and create a final draft at full size. Lightly transfer your design to the cover using one of the techniques described on page 56.

Letter over the pencil marks with a brush pen and then trace over any illustrations with appropriate markers. Once you are happy with your work, erase any pencil lines and individually fold the printer paper in half and apply pressure to crease. Punch two holes along the crease in each sheet of paper. Insert the printer paper into the kraft paper cover

As shown in the photos below, open to the center and from the inside of your journal and thread either end of your ribbon so that the ends pushed through to the outside edge. During our day of lettering, one of the moms used two ribbons and I was impressed with how beautiful it turned out. Tie your ribbon securely along the outside edge of the journal to bind it together. Trim any excess ribbon as needed.

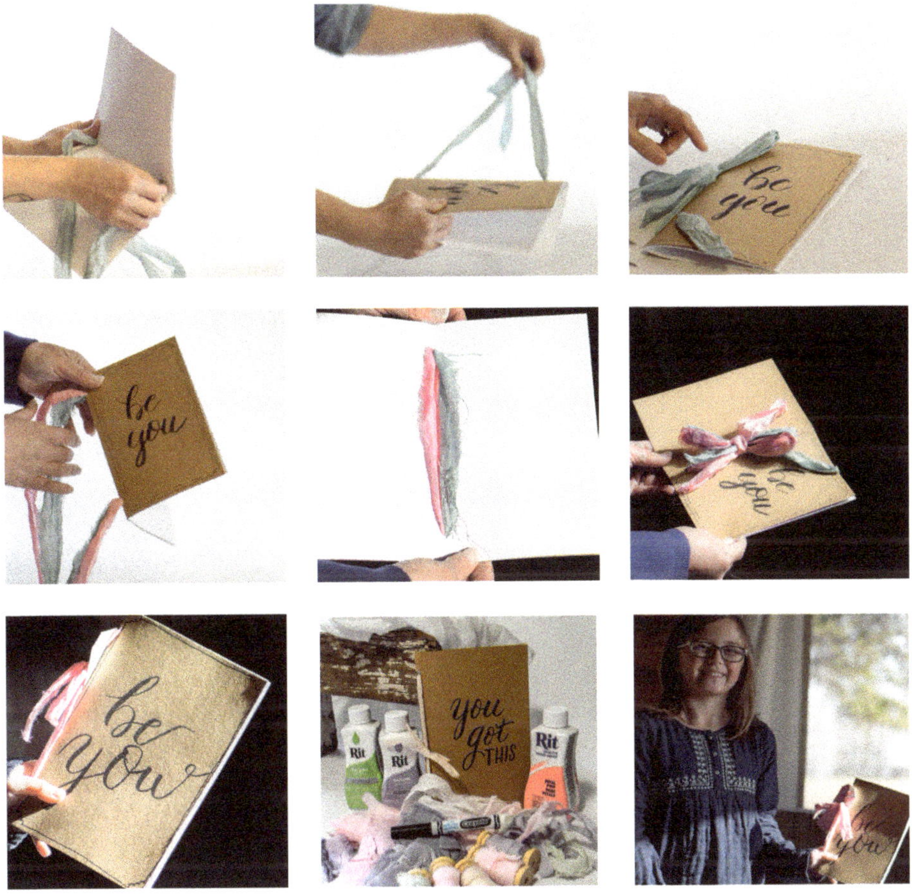

Bone folders are wonderful tools to help with papercrafts. They can be used to score and crease folds with even pressure, as well as to burnish washi tape firmly onto paper without causing rips or tears.

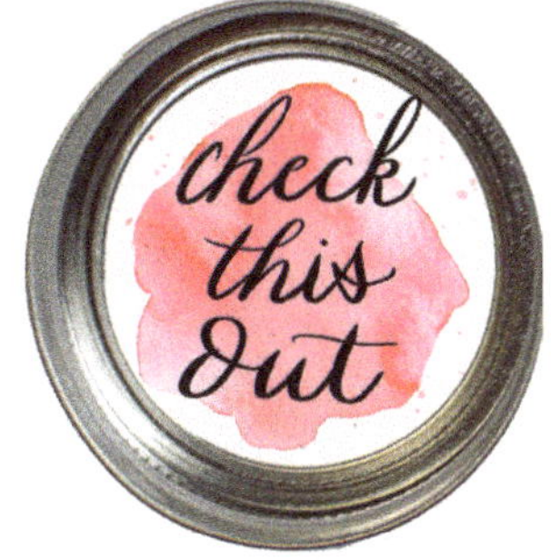

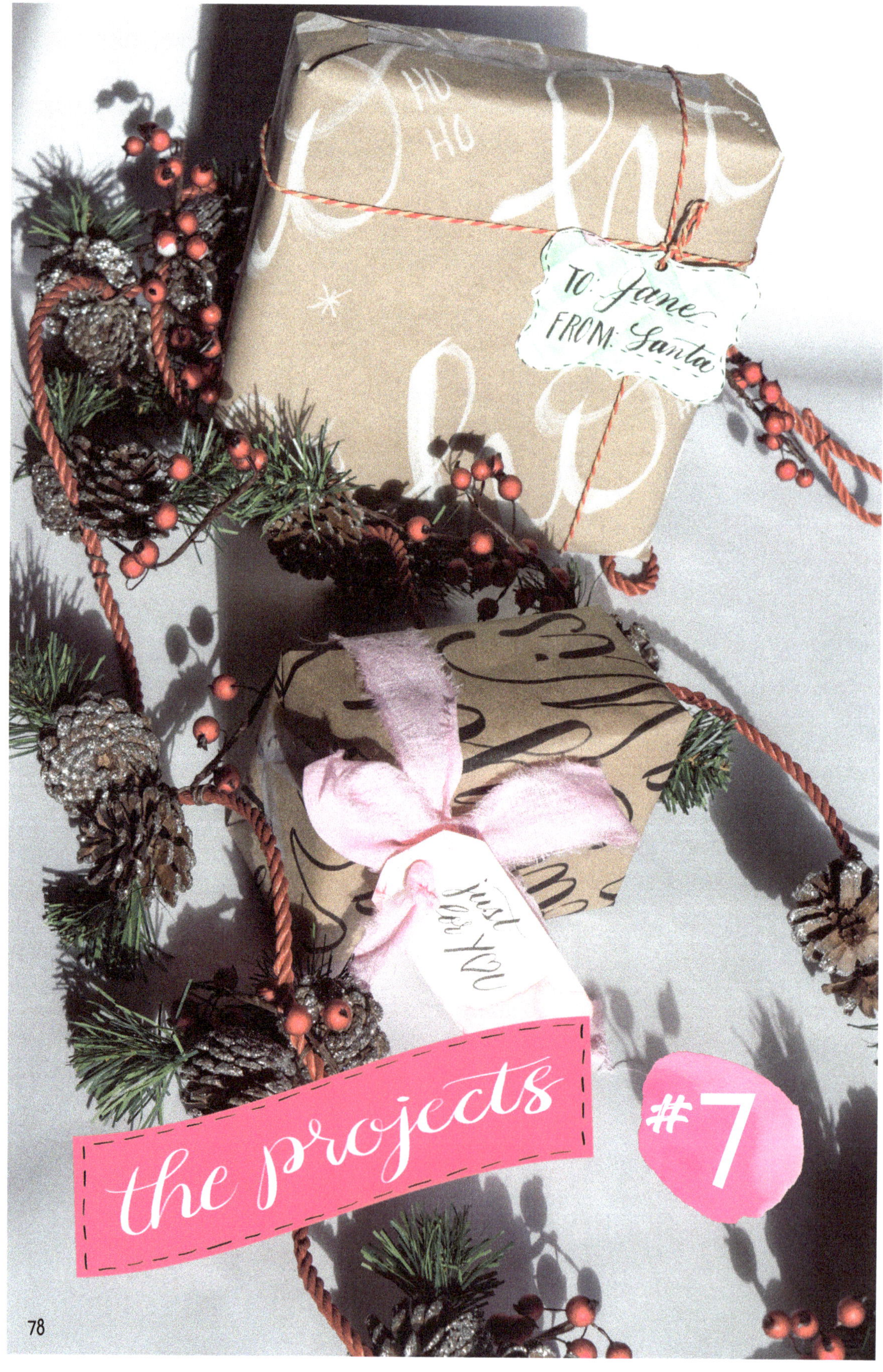
HO
HO
TO: Jane
FROM: Santa
just
for you
the projects
#7

WRAPPING PAPER

It's kraft paper to the rescue once more! I always have a roll or two in my crafting stash, because it is just so versatile. Store bought is fun, but it really doesn't take long to create a few sheets of tailor-made and hand-lettered wrapping paper, cranking your gift-giving up a notch.

SUPPLIES

- Roll of heavy duty kraft paper wrapping paper (30 inches wide by 10 feet)
- Scissors
- Black brush pen
- White, water-based extra bolt tip marker
- Pencil and eraser
- Ruler

INSTRUCTIONS

Cut kraft paper to size depending on the gift you're going to wrap and then lay the paper out on flat surface or tabletop. Choose a single word or short phrase to repeat in a pattern across the paper: Happy Birthday, Merry Christmas, No Peeking, Enjoy, For You, Make a Wish, etc.

Use a ruler to create guidelines that slant across the paper at intervals appropriate to the size of letters you'll be drawing. Remember, you'll want a blank space between the lines of lettering to avoid a confused, crunched look. Give your words some breathing space and they'll have more visual impact.

Pencil in your word or phrase, at least once per line. Feel free to have the lettering "run off" the top, bottom, and edges of the page as if the pattern extended beyond the surface your working on.

Embellish with doodles, metallic markers, gel pens, if desired and wrap your gift with the completed paper Add a bow made from a length of your hand-dyed ribbon. (see instructions page 58). Complete the hand-made look with one of your watercolour gift tags. (see instructions page 66). I hope it's helpful to see how these projects can compliment and build upon each other.

VARIATIONS

For smaller gifts, use your lettering practice sheets as wrapping paper.

MAGNETIC NOTEPADS

By now it's clear that I'm a sucker for all things stationery.

I go gaga over greeting card sets, sticky note pads, pens, pencils, markers, notepads, envelopes, scrapbooking paper, but there is one standout in my love for all things papery: magnetic notepads you put on your fridge. I adore those.

When I began designing and printing my own illustrations, creating a series of magnetic notepads was one of my first goals. Unfortunately, they're not offered by the usual small print run shops where I take my designs to be printed. At least, not within the sizes I wanted.

Which meant I had to do some investigating to see how other freelance artists were creating them and I thankfully found several methods online. After much trial and error, here's my take on creating magnetic notepads. I've included two options. The first is fairly low-tech, in that it just requires you to photocopy your final design, while the second is high-tech, as it involves scanning your design and working with it in a photo or illustration software program to create the final product.

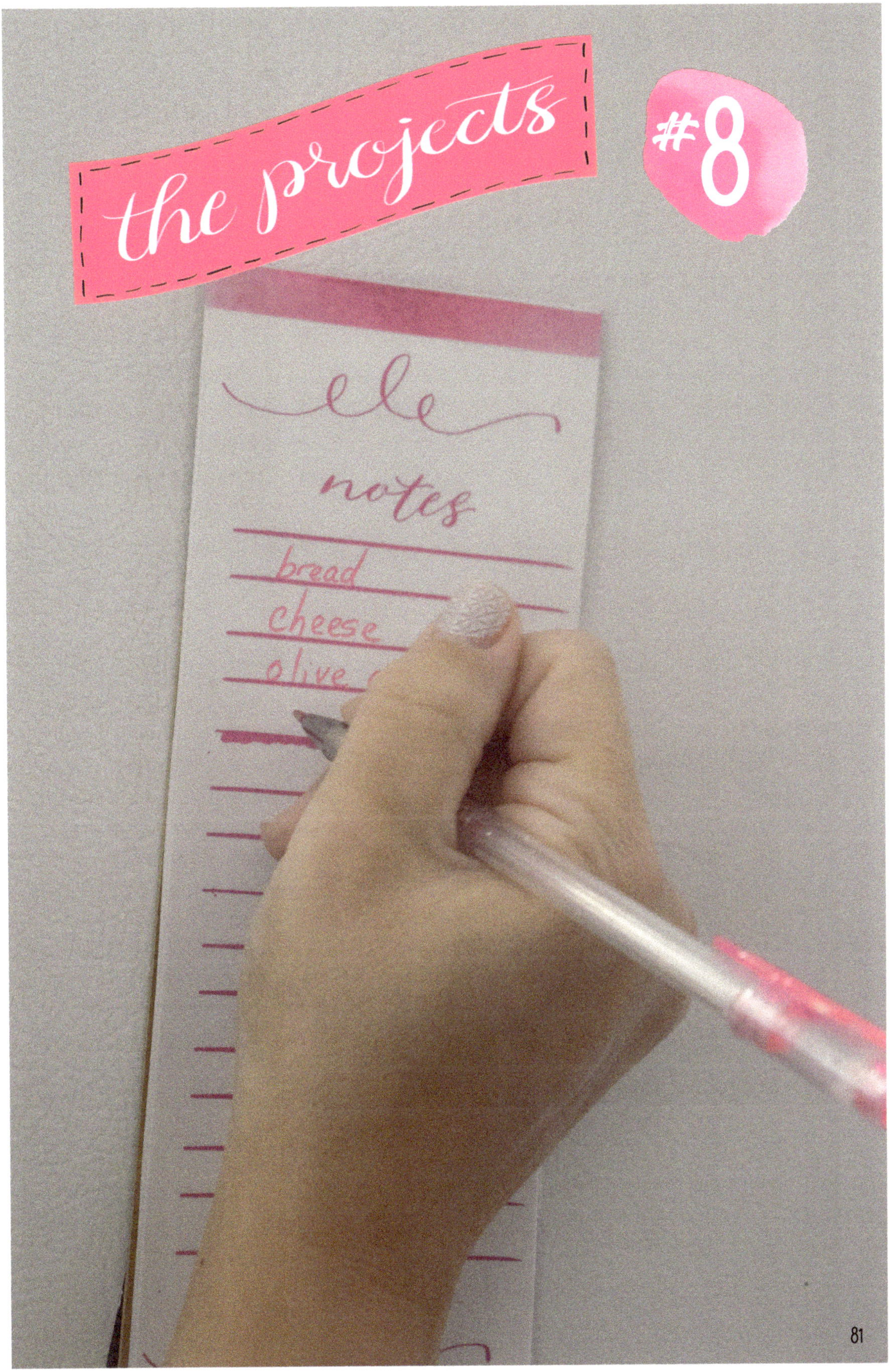

the projects #8

LOW-TECH OPTION

INSTRUCTIONS

Brainstorm the kinds of notepads you'd like to create: to do lists, grocery lists, shopping lists, Christmas gift idea lists, birthday gift idea lists. Do you want the notepads to be lined? Unlined? You could have dividers and different sections within the same notepad. Once you have a few ideas, it's time to test a few layouts

In the landscape position, fold a piece of scratch paper into three equal parts. This creates three panels, each roughly 3.5 inches wide. Each panel will be the canvas for an individual notepad.

In pencil, add your headers in lettering, rule the lines, create decorative dividers, and add different boarders.

Do this as many times as needed, you may go through several pieces of scratch paper.

SUPPLIES

- Scratch paper
- 1 sheet of 8.5x11 medium weight chip-board
- 10 sheets of white printer paper
- Mod Podge sealant
- paint brush
- 3 medium-sized bull-dog clips
- Scanner
- Printer

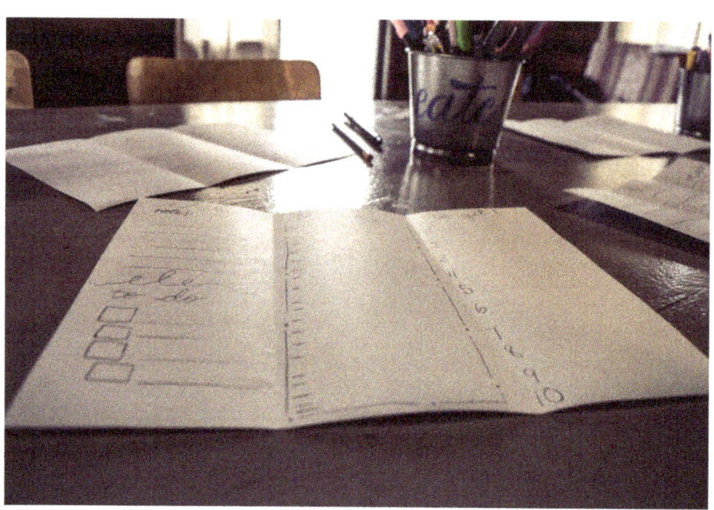

When you have three lay-outs you're happy with – one for each panel, make final drafts. Using one of the three techniques from page 56, transfer your final three layouts to a new piece of quality printer paper. Trace over your layouts with brush pens for the lettering and any other markers you may need for the boarders and illustrations you've created.

Make 10 photocopies either in colour or black and white depending on your designs. You may need to visit a local copy shop if you don't have access to a copier. With a document cutter or with scissors, cut each page along the edge of the panels so that you end up with 10 copies of each.

With a utility knife, cut the chipboard into three equal parts. These will serve as the back of our note pads. You can choose to have three notepads, each with the same designs, or you can alternate them so each notepad goes through a rotation of designs as you tear off a page.

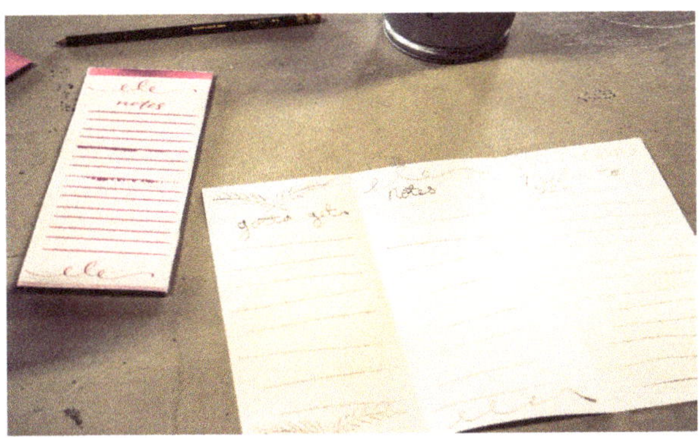

Once you have your three individual stacks of 10 pages, place them on a piece of chipboard. Add two bulldog clips to the top edges of each notepad. Line the top edge of the notepad with a layer of Mod Podge. Add a third bulldog clip at the very top center of the each notepad. Let dry.

Remove the third bulldog clip again so you can add another layer of Mod Podge across the top, then replace the third clip once more for added pressure as the Mod Podge dries. Do this three times to ensure you have a solid layer of adhesive binding the notepads together.

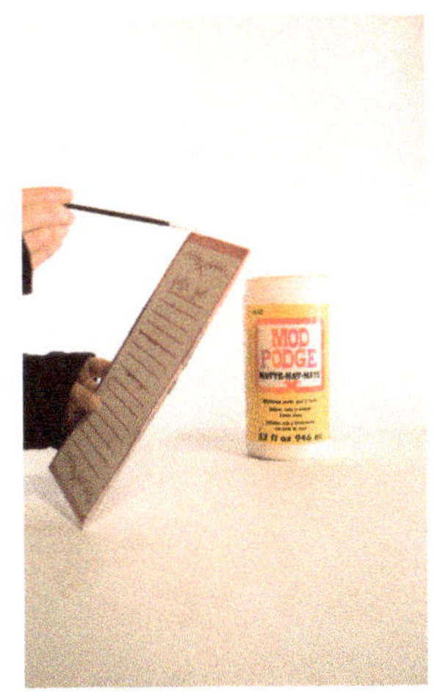

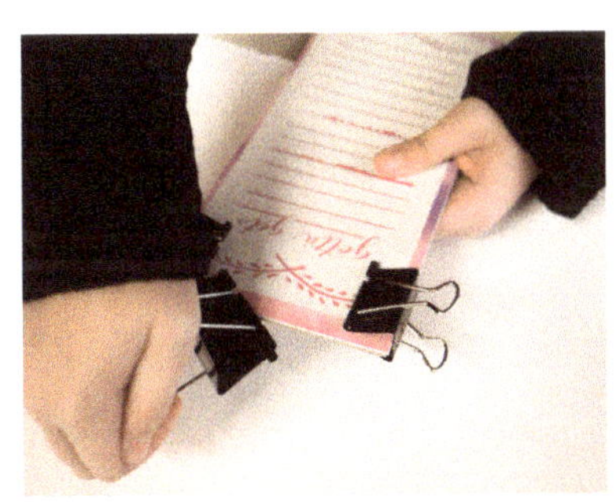

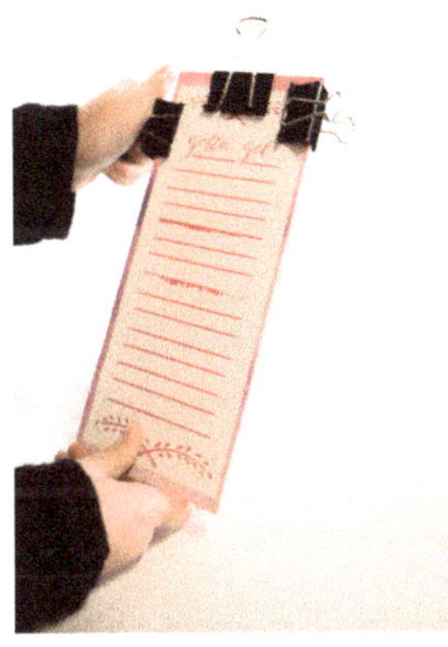

Once completely dry, remove the bulldog clips. Cut two strips of magnet tape, about 3 inches long to span most of the notepad. Fix the magnet tape strips on the chipboard backing of the notepads with one an inch from the top and the other an inch from the bottom.

Place on your fridge, filing cabinet, or any other megnetic surface.

HIGH-TECH OPTION

This option assumes you have a basic or working knowledge of how to scan, save, and manipulate images in a photo or illustration program. There are many walk-through videos and instructions online if you need help with these steps.

SUPPLIES

- Colour printer
- Scanner
- Computer or laptop
- Photo or illustration software

INSTRUCTIONS

Create several watercolour backgrounds (see instructions on page 62) and ensure they are large enough to be used as background images for your notepads.

Scan at a high resolution (at least 300 dpi) and save.

Scan your completed, final three panels and save.

In a photo editing or illustration program, create a landscape, 8.5x11 canvas and import one of your watercolour backgrounds so that it fills the canvas. This will provide a colourful and textured background for our notepad.

Add a new layer and import your scanned panel file.

Remove the white paper background. This will reveal the watercolour background on the lower layer which will leave your lettering and marker designs acting as an overlay.

Save as a high resolution jpeg file.

Print 10 copies in colour and follow the rest of the notepad assembly instructions in the low-tech option instructions.

"For me creativity
and cursive writing are
intrinsically linked. A lot
of what I do involves a
computer and keyboard, but
whenever I get stuck, I
turn to pen and paper.

There's magic that happens
when I write by hand, and
I always get the answers I
need, even if they're not quite
what I expected. So, my
advice? Trust the pen."

~Amanda Ashby,
multi-published author
and writing coach.

the projects #9

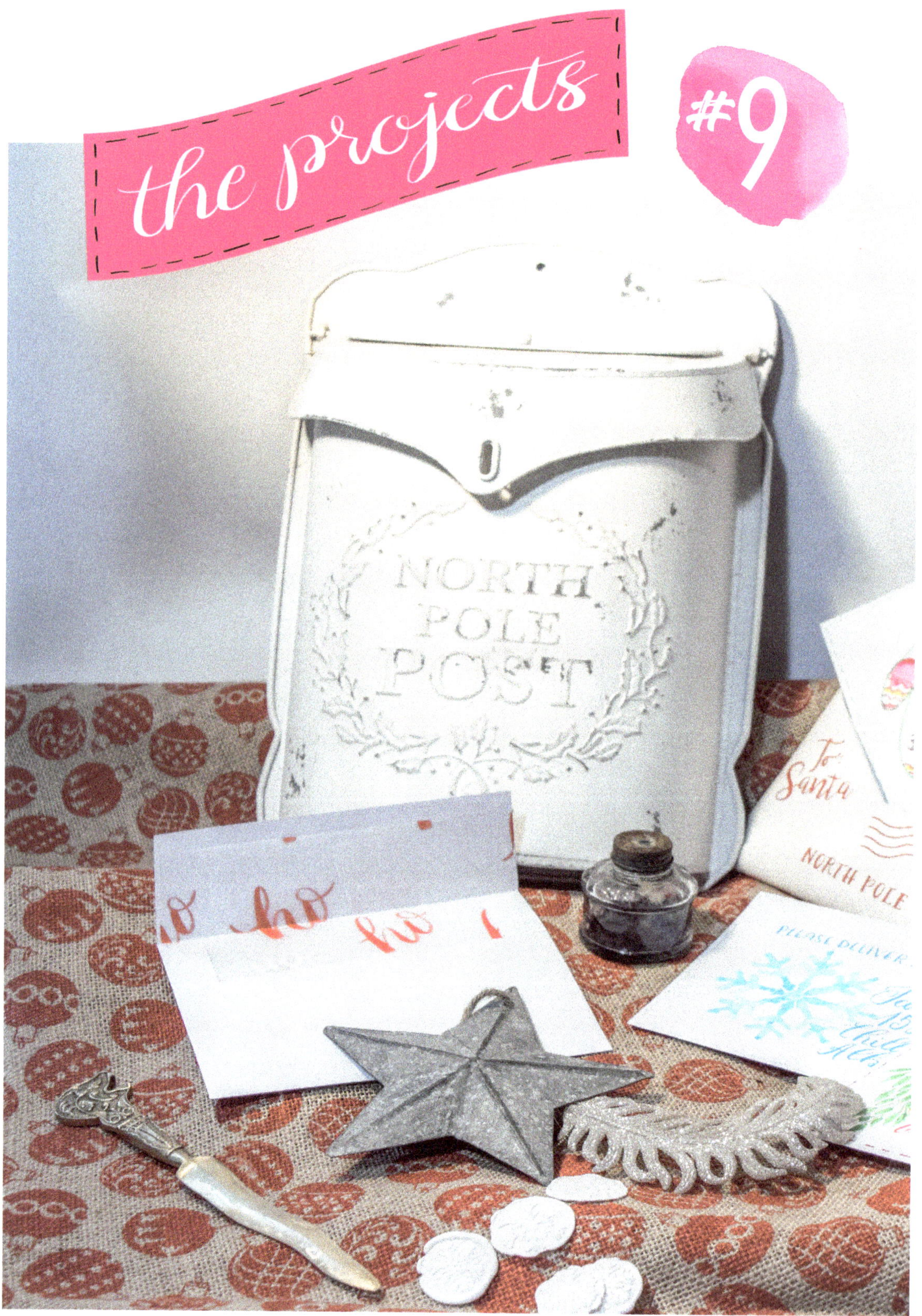

VELLUM ENVELOPE LINERS

Envelope liners can add a ton of punch to your envelopes, and they're fairly straightforward and easy to make. In this project, I've used vellum paper, but as usual, any paper that's not too thick will work. You don't want to create extra bulk to your envelope, just extra wow factor.

INSTRUCTIONS

For this festive liner we're going to use the phrase, "ho, ho, ho" in a pattern across the surface of the vellum paper following similar instructions to the wrapper paper project on page 78.

Once you're happy with your pattern, it's time to create the liner. Open your envelope and place it face down on the pattern. Decide where the best placement is so that as much of the lettering will appear on the liner as possible.

SUPPLIES

- Vellum paper (usually comes in packs of 25-50 sheets)
- Scissors
- Double-sided tape
- Envelopes
- Red brush pen
- White, water-based, extra bold tip marker

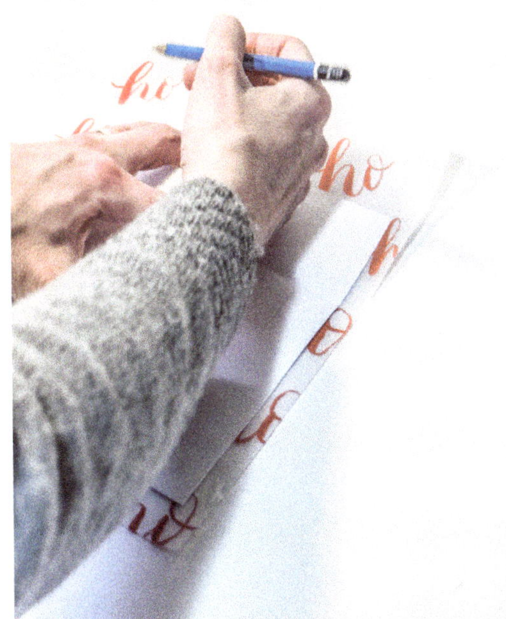

In pencil, lightly trace the outline of the envelope flap and about 2 inches along the side of the envelope onto the vellum paper.

Remove the envelop and connect the edges of your tracing with a solid line across the bottom of your liner outline.

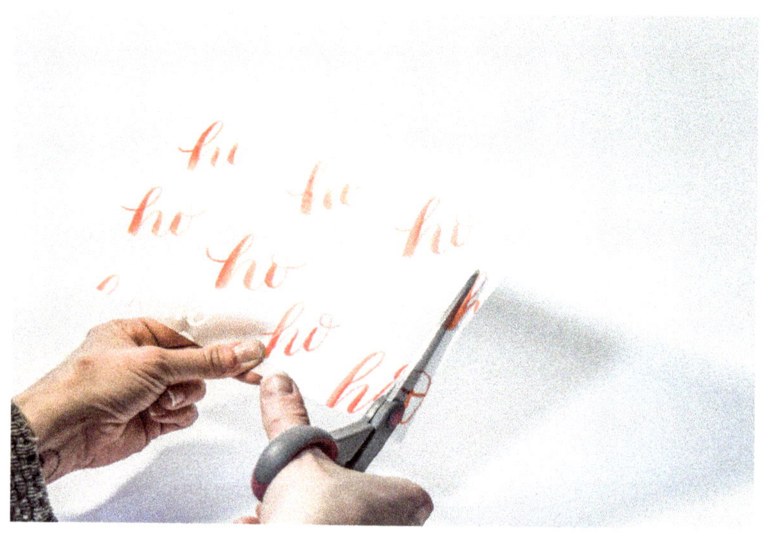

Cut out the vellum liner.
Place the vellum liner with your design facing up, inside the envelope, just under the glue line on the envelope flap.
Fold the envelope and reinforce the crease with pressure on the edge. A bone folder would work well here.

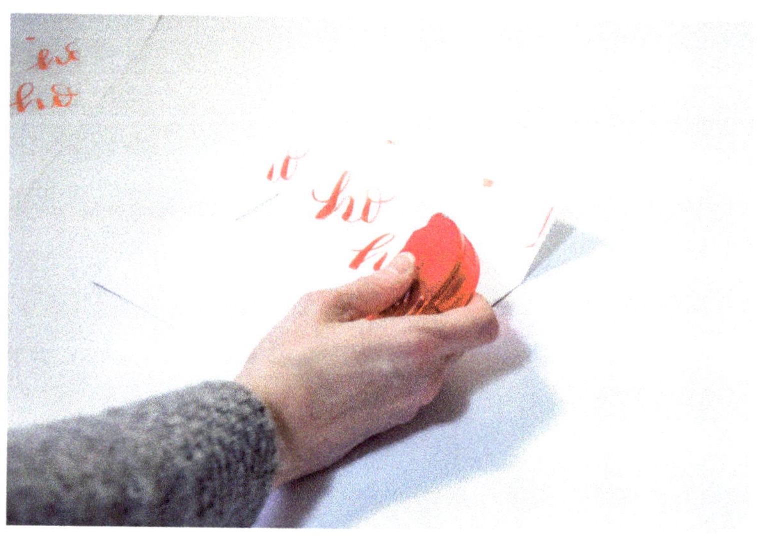

You may need to slightly trim the edges so that the liner easily fits into the envelope and doesn't cause any buckling.
Fix the liner in place with a few strips of double sided tape.

VARIATIONS

Create a watercolour background or any doodle or illustration. Scan and tweak in a photo or illustration program, perhaps creating a pattern or add layers of illustrations as needed. Print, cut, and adhere in the envelope as with the instructions above.

Doodle, paint, or draw directly on the black space inside the envelope to act as an instant liner. Note that some markers will bleed through the front of the envelope, so be sure to do a test first.

Create a liner from scrapbook paper, wrapping paper, your lettering practice sheets, newspaper clippings, etc. Sky's the limit as long as it can be cut to size and doesn't bulk up your envelope.

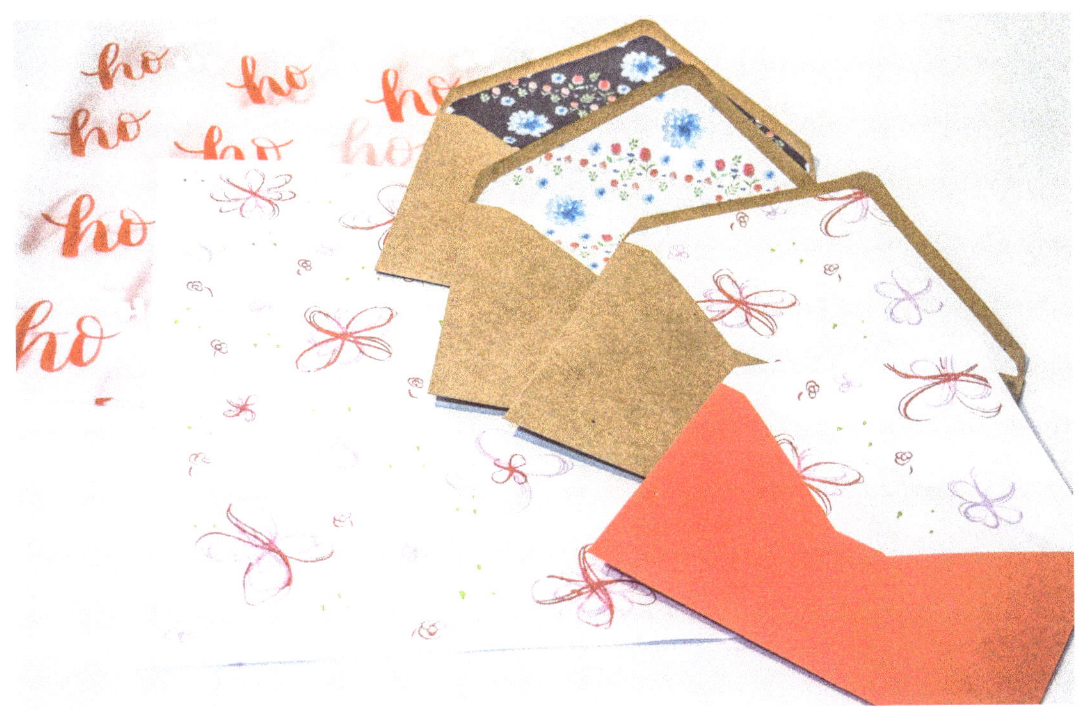

cool tip

Envelope liners are supposed to be a bit random and quirky.

If you don't feel you've captured as much of the design as you wanted, grab a new piece of vellum paper and recreate your pattern with whatever adjustments are needed.

RUSTIC CHRISTMAS ORNAMENTS

This is a wonderful activity to do with your family to create ornaments you'll treasure for a lifetime.

INSTRUCTIONS

Choose a few words or phrases you'd like to letter on the ornaments and plan your design on some scratch paper. Remember you can convey different moods with the style of lettering you choose. All caps for drama, airy and flowing for an inspirational feel, etc.

Decide if you're going to have a decorative border – dashes, or holly leaves and berries – incorporate this into your sketches. Once you have a few solid designs, create final versions and transfer them to wood ornaments using the graphite or pencil method described on page 56.

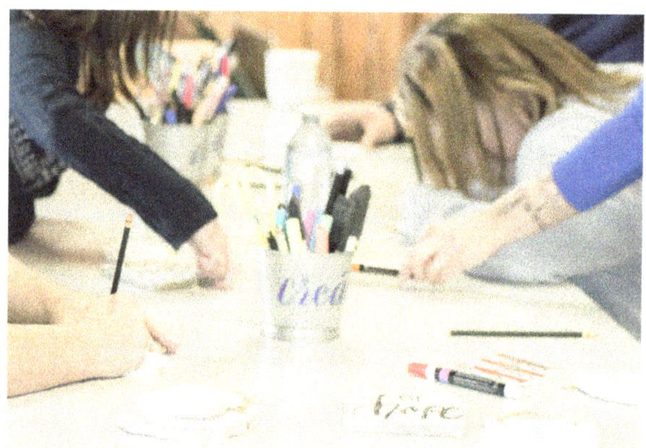

Trace your design with the oil-based markers. Note that these take time to dry and be careful not to smudge your work or accidentally cause the colours to bleed together. If necessary, complete your lettering first, wait for it to dry and then work on the boarder.

Allow at least an hour to dry, and then spray with a light mist of glitter for additional sparkle. A light coat of matte sealer will ensure your ornament will withstand being repeatedly hung on a tree and then packed away at the end of each season.

SUPPLIES

- Raw wood ornament shapes (or ones already primed and sanded for a rustic appearance. Either type should already come with a twine loop for hanging. If not, you can easily cut twine, create a loop, and glue the ends to the back of the ornament with some Mod Podge and light pressure.10 sheets of blank or lined printer paper)
- Oil-based bullet tip markers in festive colours (black, gold, red, green, silver, etc.)
- Scratch paper
- Pencil and eraser
- Glitter spray
- Matte spray sealer

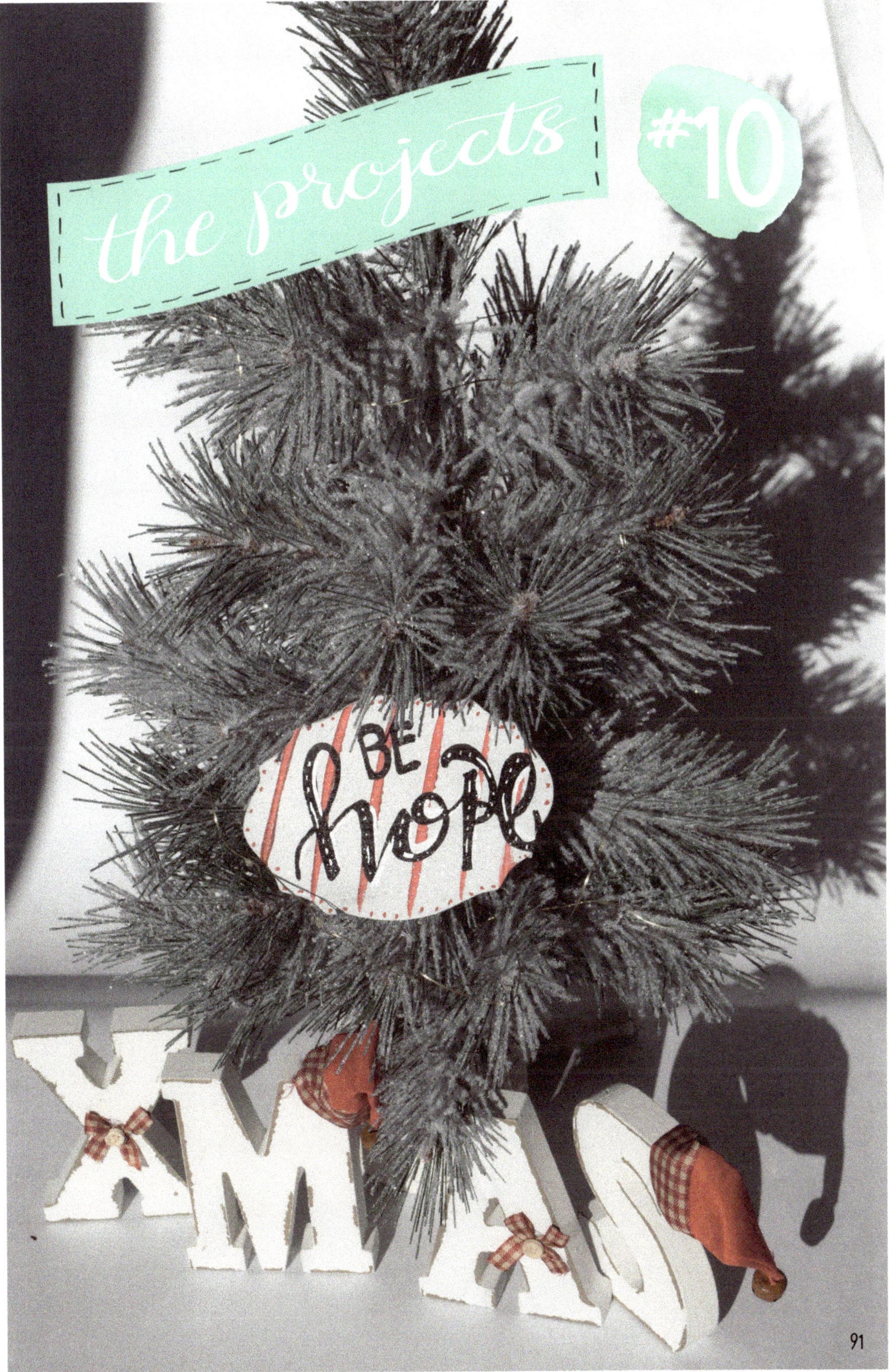

the projects
#10
BE hope
XMAS

the projects #11

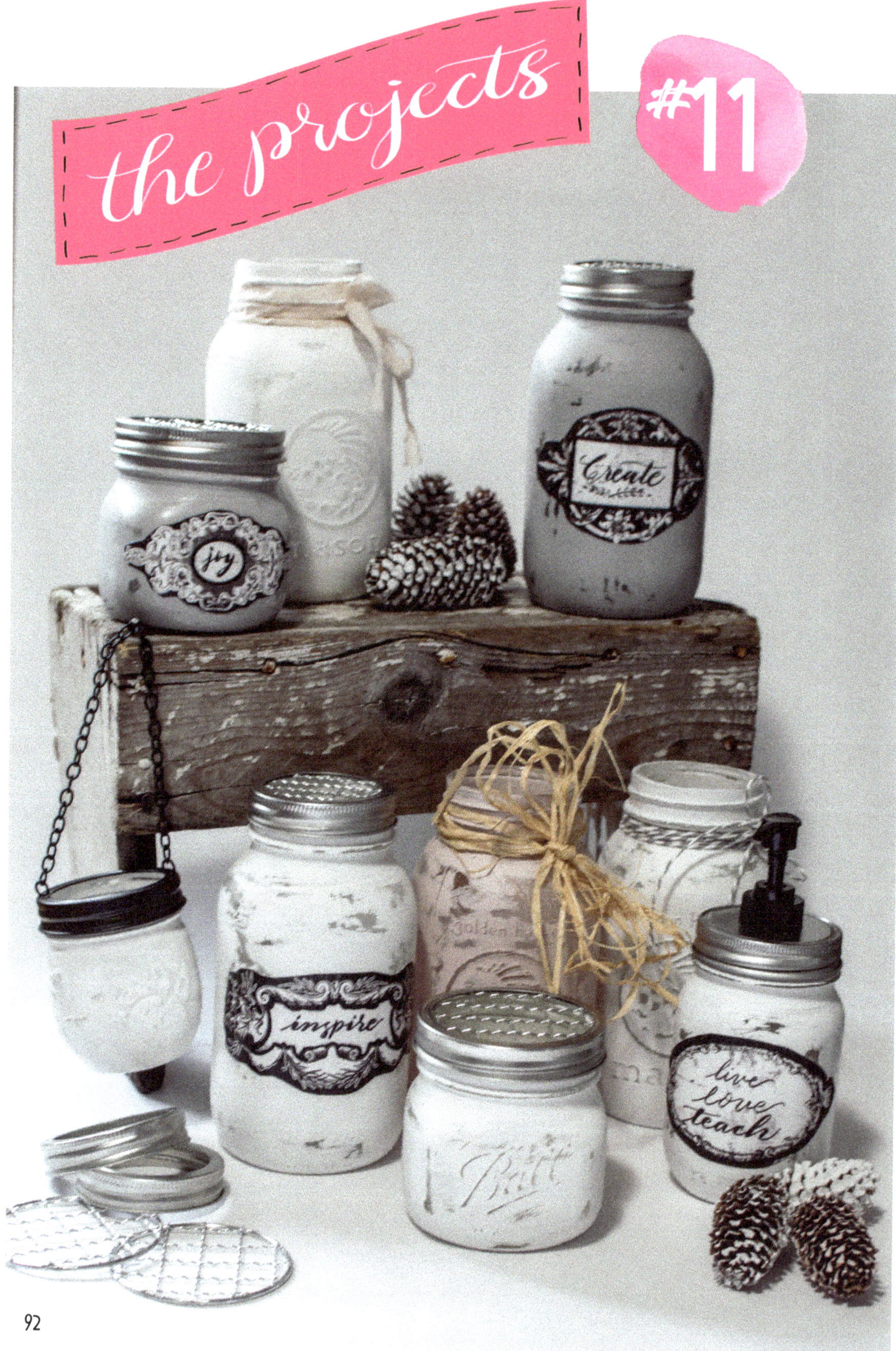

CHALK-PAINTED MASON JARS

Ah, the mason jar, holder of food preserves displayed on dark, creepy basement cold-room shelves since 1858. I think John Landon Mason would be amazed at how versatile his glass jar home-canning invention has become. Mason jars have come into the light in a big way.

They are great for centre pieces at weddings and special events, flower vases, toothbrush holders, soap dispensers, salt shakers, lanterns and chandeliers, containers for craft supplies, containers for dry goods, snow globes, smoothie and beverage drinking glasses - the list is endless.

Possibly my favourite incarnation is the chalk-painted mason jar. There's something about these hand-painted and lightly distressed jars, with their vintage vibe and creamy pastel hues that radiate warmth and comfort. The bonus – you can customize the look to suit any occasion, holiday, or colour palette.

This makes them wonderful home décor pieces and an excellent choice for gift-giving.

This project is exactly that, a fun-to-do family activity that produces the perfect thank you to that special someone in your life, such as, a teacher. Who better to treat with a home-made gift than the kind of person who keeps on giving? I work part time in an elementary school library and my husband is a high school teacher. Believe me, I know a home-made treasure like this would be a greatly appreciated, any time of the year pick me up.

SUPPLIES

- Light-grey chalk paint
- Sponge brushes
- Paint stir stick
- Clear poly, or some kind of material to protect your painting surface
- Matte spray sealer
- Mod Podge
- Fine grit sanding sponge
- Mason jars of various sizes
- Mason jar accessories: pump insert lid, black chain hanging lid, wire jar lid

NOTE: This project takes a bit of patience to complete, as the chalk-paint must dry for at least 24 hours. With that in mind, it might work best as a weekend effort, with one day for painting/drying and the next for sanding and adding embellishments.

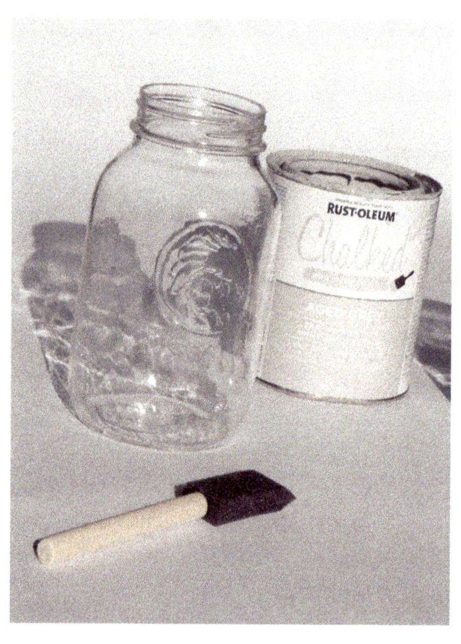

INSTRUCTIONS

You can repurpose jars you already have around your house but be sure to give them a good cleaning, removing any labels and residue, and let thoroughly dry. New jars are ready to go out of the box.

Stir your chalk paint well and select a table or work space that you can occupy with the jars for a few days as they dry. Cover your work surface with poly or something to protect it from spills

Using a sponge brush, paint two coats over the entire outer surface of each jar, allowing paint to dry between coats. Rest each jar on its mouth to dry.

Let dry for at least 24 hours. While it's tempting to skip this step, it really is crucial to the final result. If you don't allow the chalk paint to fully dry, it won't cure to the glass and when you attempt to sand or decoupage other elements, the chalk paint will rub off.

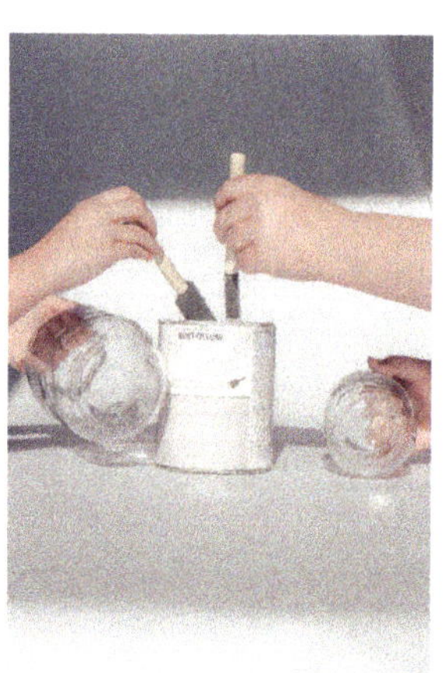

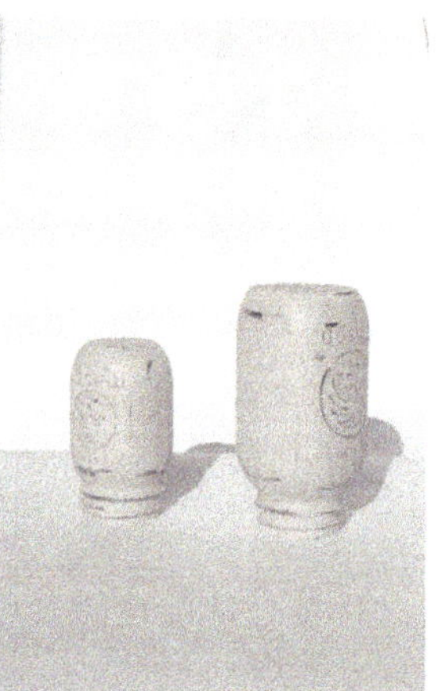

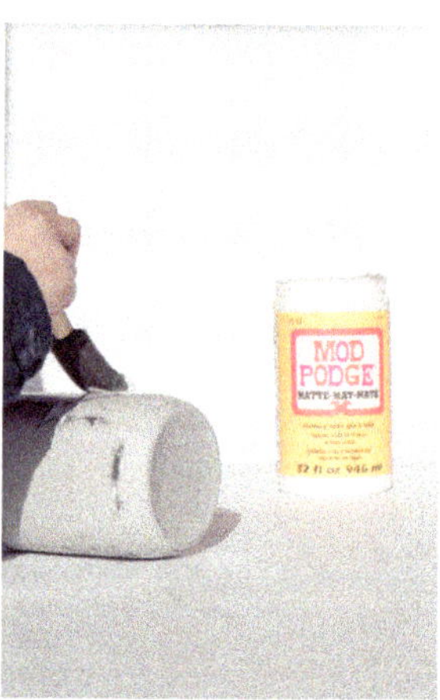

While you wait, use the templates on page 114 to print and cut out, or help you design your own mason jar label which we will decoupage onto the jars when dry.

Choose a word or phrase you'd like to letter in the blank space provided in the template labels. Practice on scratch paper and transfer to the blank label using one of the transfer methods mentioned on page 56. Letter with a brush pen and cut out.

To prevent the label ink from bleeding when we decoupage it on the jar, give it a fine mist of the matte sealing spray and let dry for several minutes. Once dry, lightly sand around the mouth threads, the Ball Mason text and/or any details on the glass you wish to feature. You can also lightly sand "highlights" around the jar – on the shoulders and rounded edges to give a rustic and aged appearance. Less is more, however, so don't overwork this step.

Using the Mod Podge, decoupage your label on the smooth side of the jar. You may need to press the label down and hold it for a few seconds in spots that don't immediately glom onto the chalk paint. Let dry for fifteen to twenty minutes.

Spray jars with matte spray sealer. Do a few coats if the jars are likely to be exposed to moisture as with lotion, soap, or toothbrush holders. Dry completely.

Thread on the appropriate lid for each jar. Note that the wire lids work well on the quart jars for holding flower arrangements or the pint jars for toothbrush holders. Pint jars are also just the right size for the pump inserts to hold hand lotion or liquid soap, and the black chain hanging lids work exceptionally well on the half-pint round jam jars as mini lanterns with battery operated tea lights for convenience and safety.

VARIATIONS

Wrap your own hand-dyed ribbon (see instructions on page 58), raffia, twine or other material around the top of the jar.

Paint the jars according to a holiday or theme: Christmas, fall or spring colours, TARDIS blue with a red bowtie (can you tell I'm a Doctor Who fan?), use gold or silver spray paint instead of chalk paint for a more formal feel, etc.

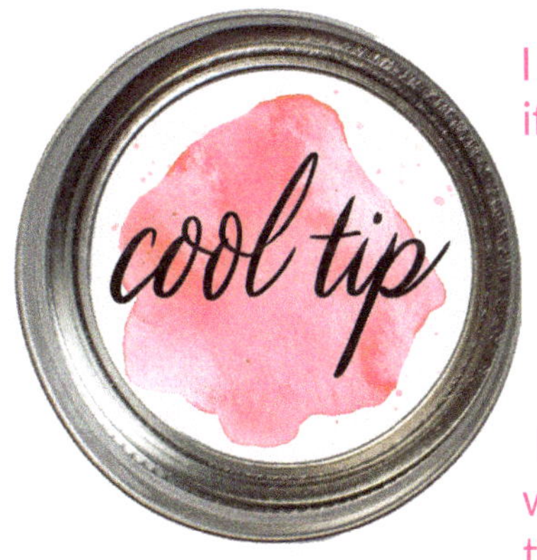

I find it helpful to fit the jar around one hand as if it's a mitten and then paint from the base of the jar to the mouth. Later you can paint the rim of the jar if you're not going to use the metal twist lids, but it isn't necessary if your lid covers the rim.

Be sure to clean your sponge brushes with warm, soapy water and rinse well. Squeeze out the excess moisture and let the brush dry in an upright position. All paint brushes should be stored this way to prevent the bristles or tips from damage and warping out of shape. With proper care of your brushes, you'll be able to reuse them many times.

EMBOSSED CERAMIC MUGS

I live in Cold Lake, Alberta, a city of approximately 15, 000 souls, high in the Canadian north. Yes, the lake is big. Yes, it's cold. We have snow eight months of the year, with winter temperatures reaching record lows of -53 °C.

You'd think I would be sick of being cold, but even during our short summers, I find myself longing for a cool, fall day. I adore sweater weather.

I also believe there's nothing quite like a marshmellowy mug of hot chocolate on a cold day. Combining these two truths in a lettering project made the utmost sense to me.

SUPPLIES

- White ceramic mugs
- Black embossing pen (You can use a clear ink pen, but it will make seeing your lettering a bit tricky)
- Embossing powders (Here I'm using a pink powder infused with sparkles for texture which will emulate a fuzzy sweater, and a regular silver powder)
- Static pad
- Scratch paper
- Embossing heat tool
- Small paintbrush
- Coffee filter

INSTRUCTIONS

If you're using a new mug, it should be good to go but if not, be sure to clean your mug and let it dry thoroughly. Examine your mug and decide on the best placement for your "Sweater Weather" lettering, or lettering of your choice, so that it has the most visibility.

For this final project, I'm encouraging you to work freehand, without a lettering template. Use the lettering visible in the photos as a general guide. Practice on scratch paper to perfect your work.

If your embossing pen is dual tipped, use the brush tip for the "Sweater" lettering and the bullet tip for the "WEATHER" lettering, which is in all caps. If your embossing pen is a bullet tip only, use the fauxligraphy technique mentioned on page 16 to create the "Sweater" lettering and simple, monoline capitals for the "WEATHER" text with no need to add weight to the downstrokes.

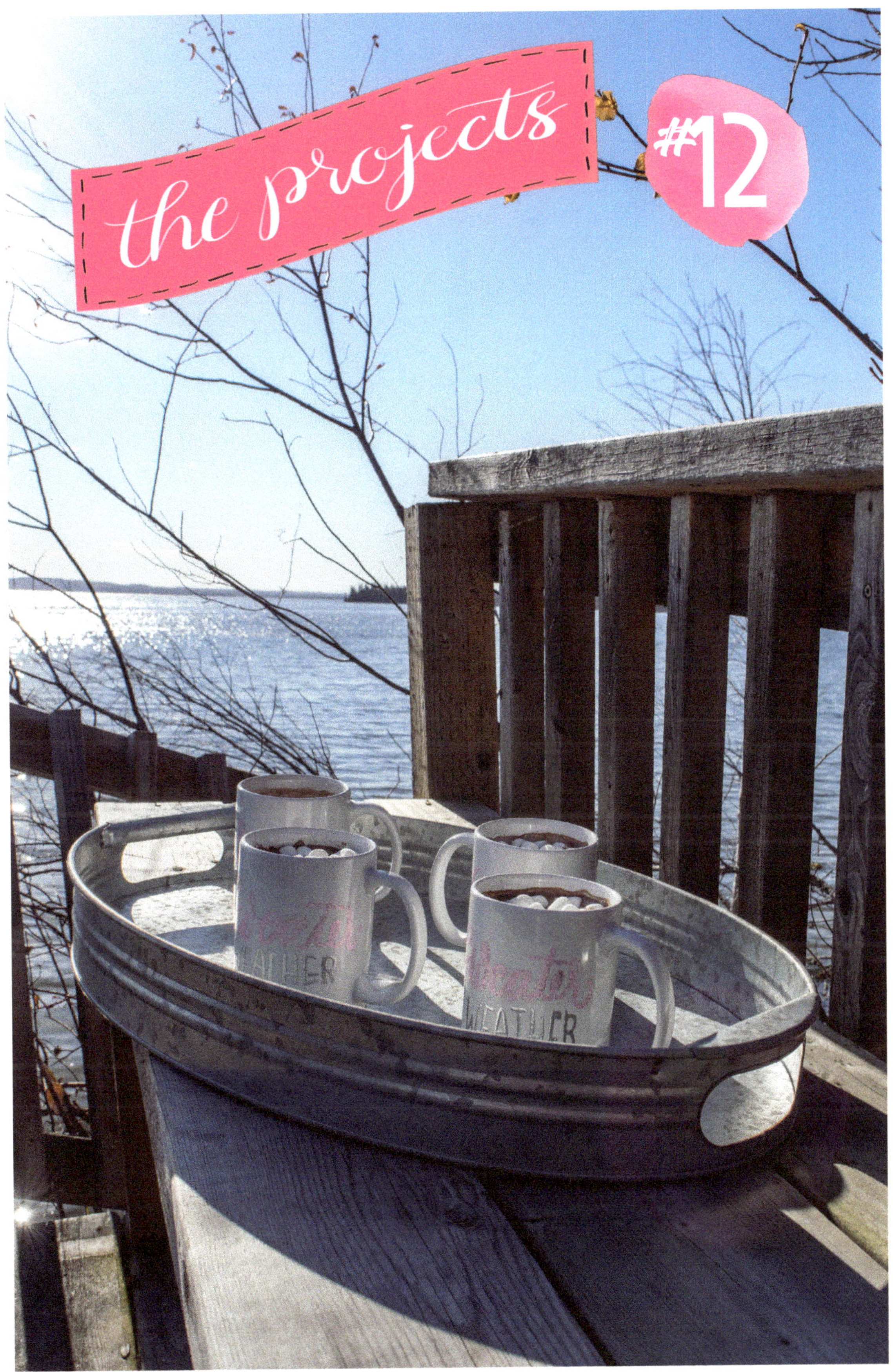
the projects
#12

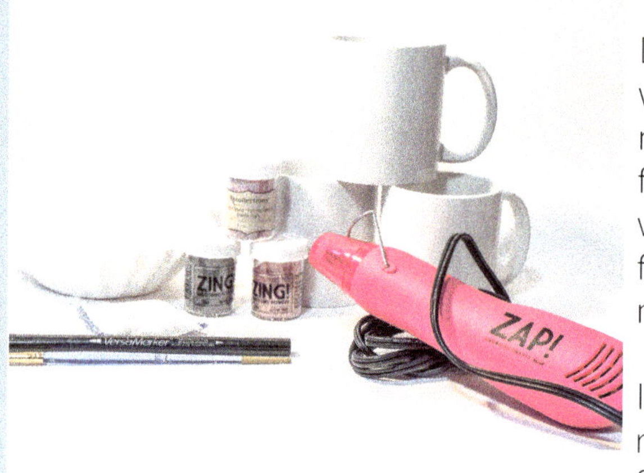

Don't worry if you make an error, this ink will wipe off – you'll just need to give the mug a good cleaning to remove any traces for the final version. Hold the mug as if you were sipping from it and evaluate your reflection in a mirror. (Oh, you look amazing, my friend!)

Ignore the fact that your words will appear reversed; you're just concerned with the following: Are the words centered, both vertically and horizontally on the mug? In other words, are they too high up or hugging the bottom too much? Do you need to make the words bigger or smaller?

Your mug may be larger or smaller than the template I've provided. Are the individual letters too crowded together? Keep in mind the embossing will thicken up your lines and possibly make cramped letters illegible.

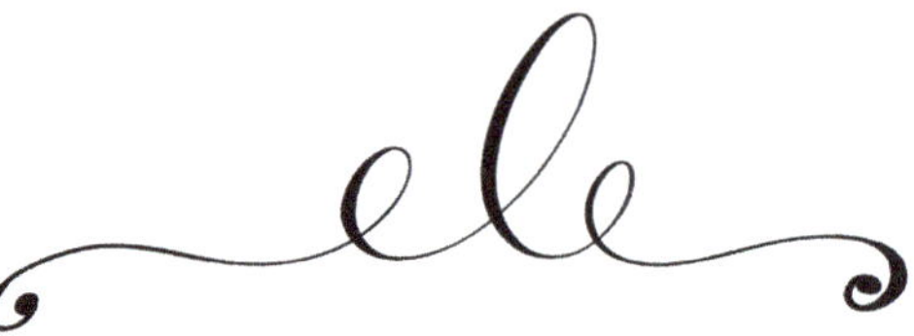

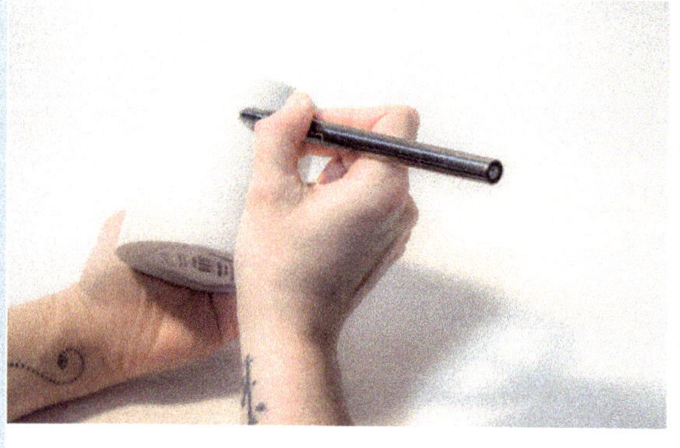

When you're happy with how it looks, wipe off the ink for the "WEATHER" lettering. We're just going to do one colour / word at a time. You'll also have to trace over the "Sweater" lettering again with your pen before you add the embossing powder, as the ink must be wet for the power to stick.

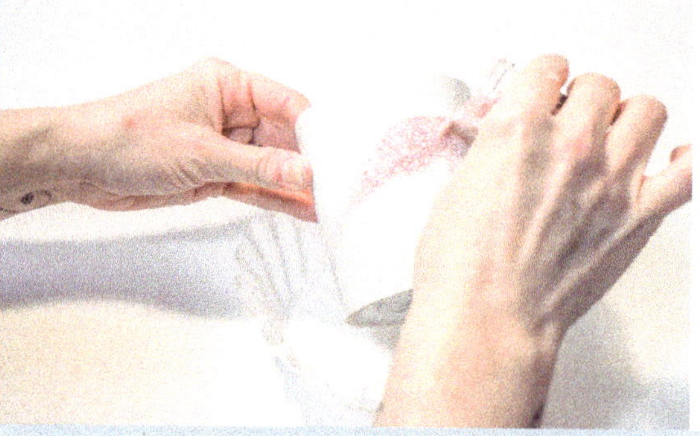

Holding the mug over the open coffee filter, pour the pink embossing powder over the word "Sweater".

Using your embossing heat tool, apply the hot air to the embossing powder until cured. As a general suggestion you could use plastic tongs to hold mug so as not to burn your fingers, also start at one end of the letter and work the heat to the other as you see the embossing powder melt.

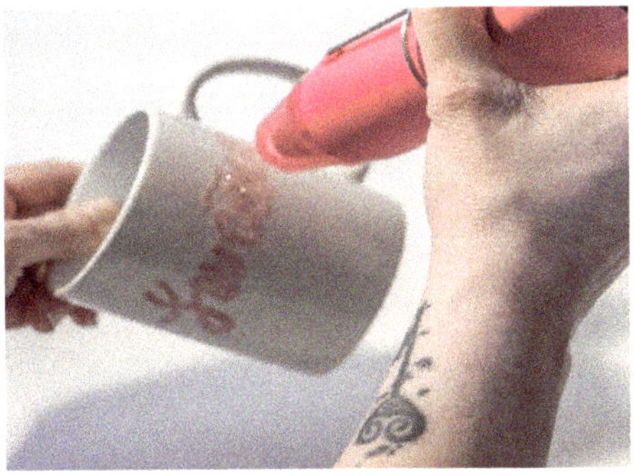

Let the mug cool.

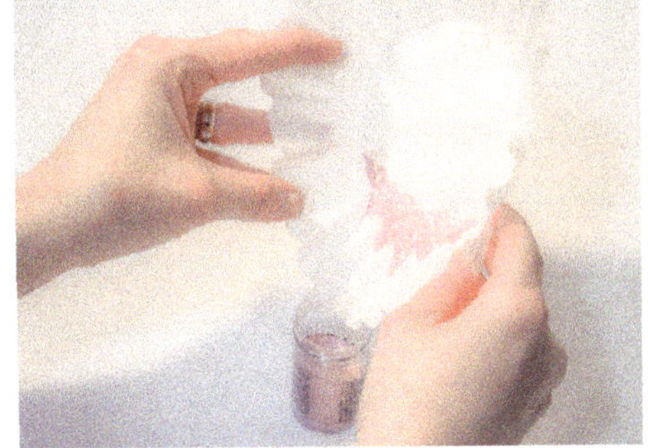

Curve the coffee filter and gently guide the left-over powder back into the container for future use.

Follow the same method for adding the "WEATHER" text to your mug with the embossing pen, but this time you can be much looser as it is an informal, all caps look.

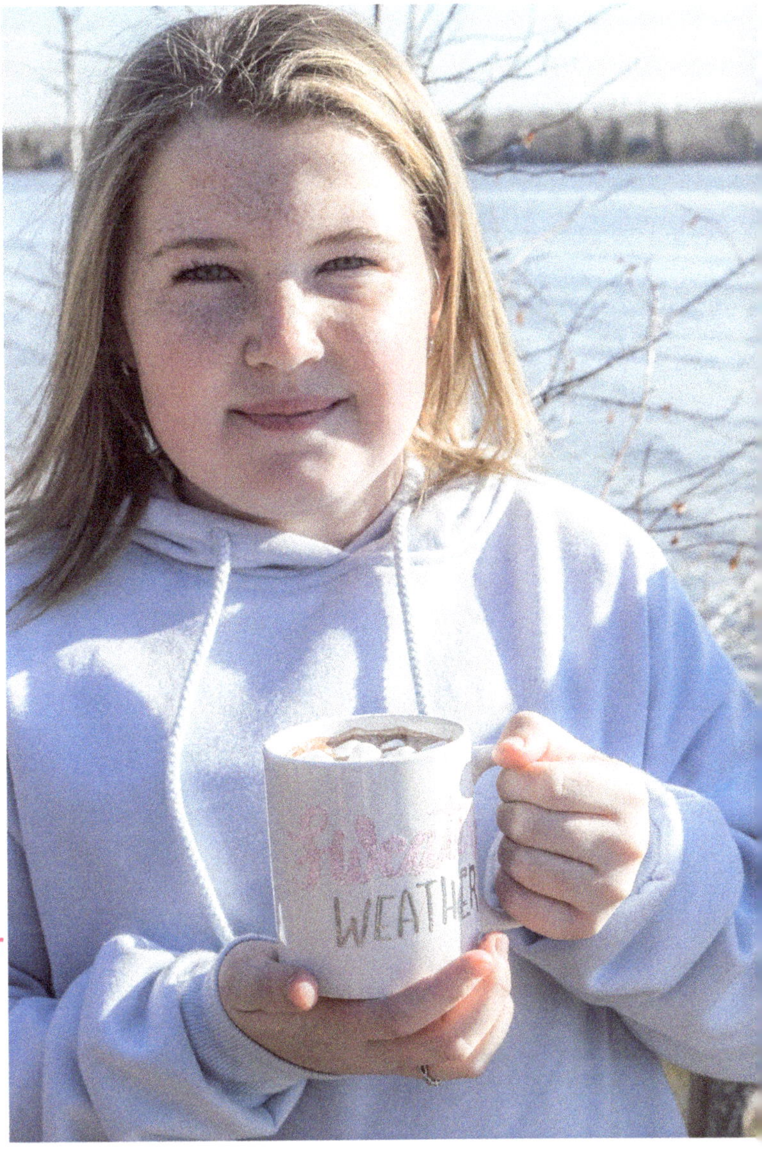

Follow the same instructions to emboss with the grey embossing powder.

Return remainders back into the container.

NOTE: Embossing heat tools can burn skin very quickly if you're not careful. Follow the instructions that came with your tool for safety purposes.

NOTE: These mugs are NOT dishwasher or microwave safe. Gently hand-wash and let air dry. With repeated use, the embossing will start to fade over time.

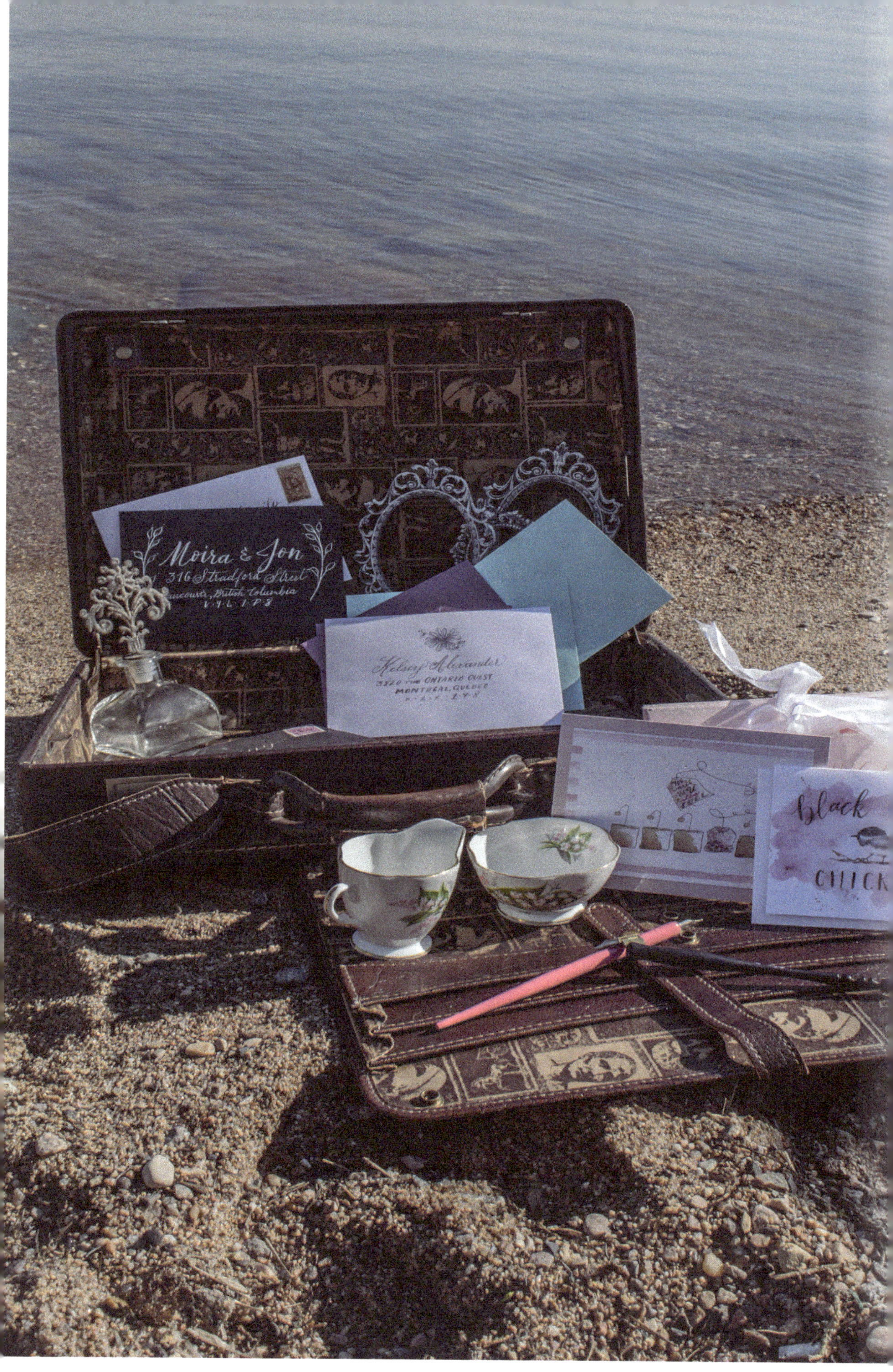
Moira & Jon
316 Stradford Street
British Columbia
Kelsey Alexander
Black

HAPPY MAIL THE LOST ART OF LETTER WRITING

There's a growing movement to bring cursive and letter writing back to the world, known as Happy Mail.

For some it can be care packages to loved ones, mail exchanges between friends or pen pals, or simply a way to spread some joy. For me, Happy Mail is a combination of all those things, as well as a way to make my lettering practice purposeful, mindful, and by doing this on a regular basis (I send Happy Mail to 5 different people each month through a random draw on my Facebook page), it also holds me accountable to my practice.

Okay, this thing sounds intriguing, but you're probably asking ... how do I start?

With some planning.

Letters can be written as short and sweet messages, a jam-packed single page, or fill several pages with all your thoughts, and hopes, and dreams. There's no right or wrong way to compose a letter. However, thanks to the speed and handiness of email and text messaging, most of us haven't actually sat down to hand write and then send a letter off in the mail - in a very long time. Or ever.

Just the idea of physically writing a letter might seem overwhelming. We may find ourselves struggling with how to begin, what to write, or once we're scrawling away - how to wrap things up.

As a writer who relies heavily on plot and story structure outlines – I find it helpful to spend some time thinking about what I'd like to cover in a letter, what questions I can ask, or information I'm keen to share. This is the beauty of letter writing. It requires more thought and personal investment than simply firing off a rapid text or email. The time you spend before you write a single word will pay off in the end when you've created a cohesive Happy Mail experience for your recipient or reader.

To do this, start with a central theme. This ties your letter together for your recipient – from the actual content you write about in you letter or greeting card, to the envelope art, addressing style, the wax seal you select, to any other Happy Mail goodies you include, such as letter confetti - stickers, small artwork, watercolour cutouts, or other small treasures discovered when the envelope is opened.

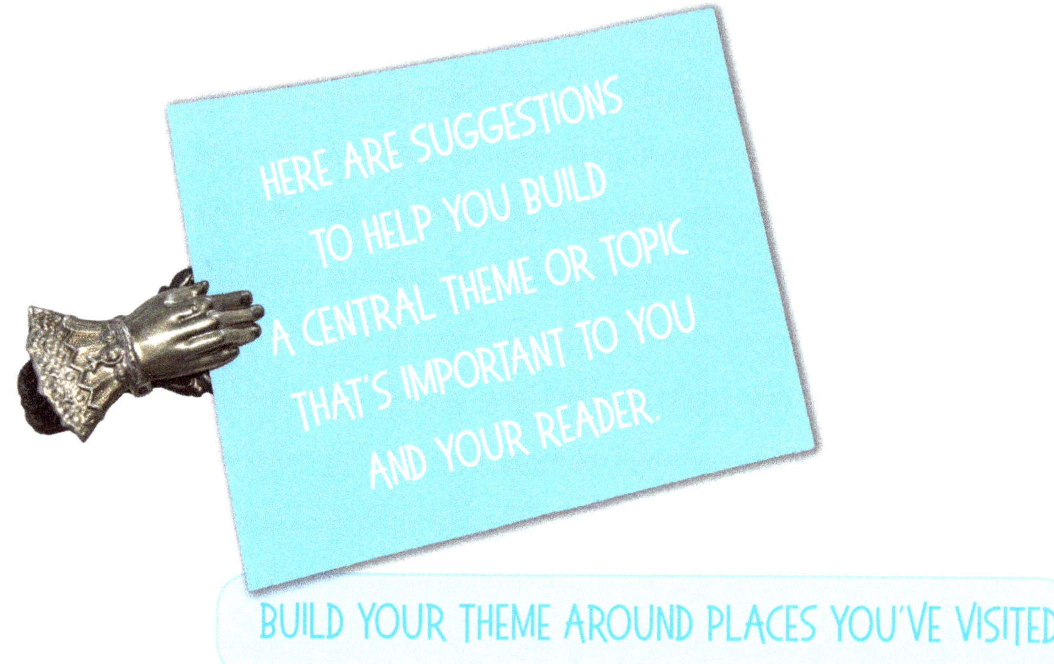

BUILD YOUR THEME AROUND PLACES YOU'VE VISITED

If you've done some traveling recently, why not virtually take your reader their with a letter that will make them feel like they were along for the journey.

Maybe you've been on a cruise, spent time at a beachy hot spot, gone mountain climbing, visited cities in Europe or Asia, or you've explored an area in your country that you've never been to before ... all of these experiences are rich fodder for theme building and letter writing.

Maybe your reader hasn't had the opportunity to visit you where you live, or hasn't visited in many years. Why not welcome them or reintroduce them to your hometown or city by featuring the things about it that you love best?

These are just a few ideas you can use or that may spark ideas of your own. You could do an entire series of letters with each one exploring a slightly different topic that still relates to the overall theme.

One letter a month featuring a different vintage-style candy for example... cinnamon hearts for February, lollipops for December, etc. Once you've selected a theme, go through this checklist to find additional elements.

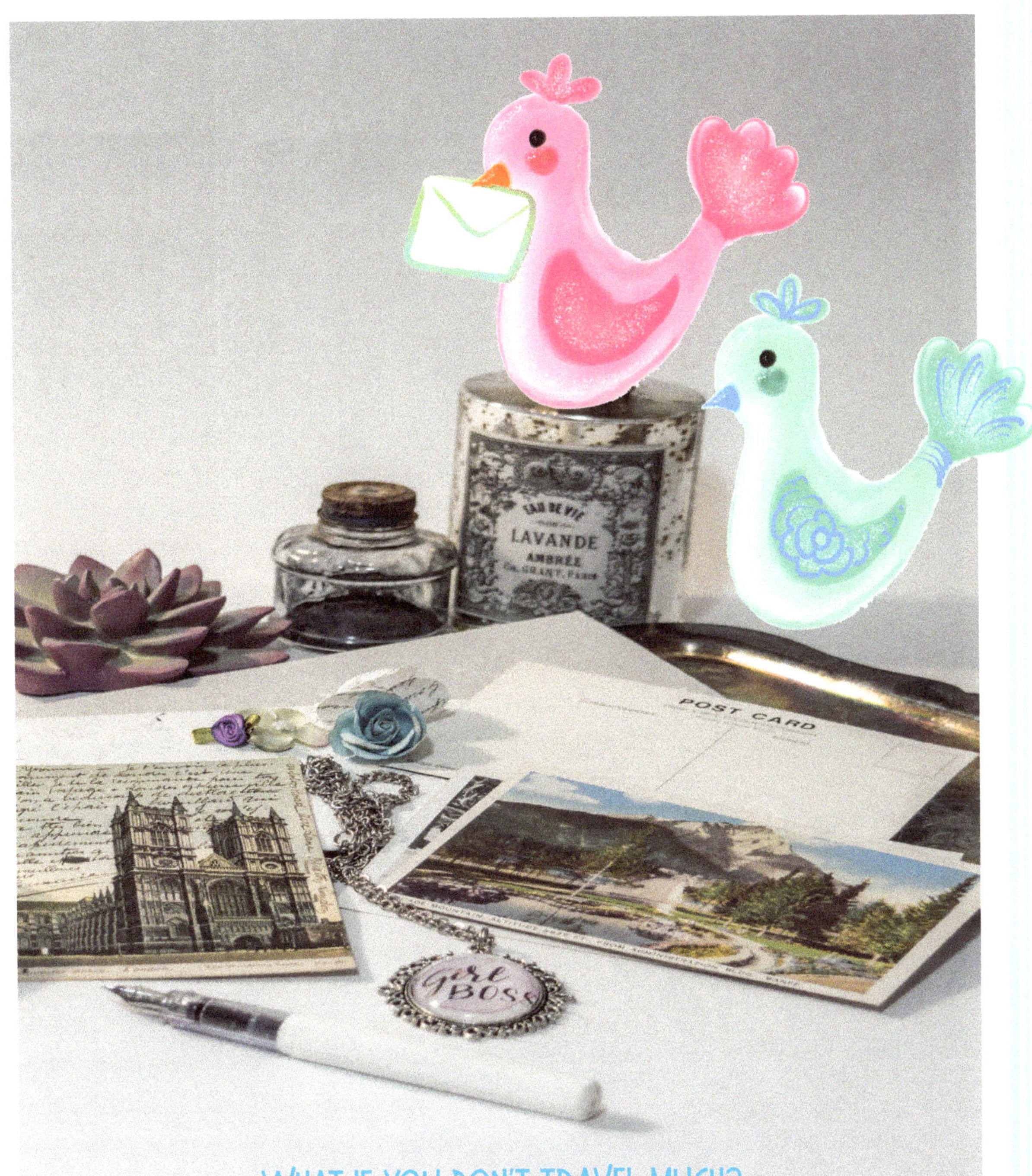

WHAT IF YOU DON'T TRAVEL MUCH?

Take a few minutes to think of all the wonderful things to see and do, just by stepping out your own front door.

There are always elements of home that are unique and worthy of attention.

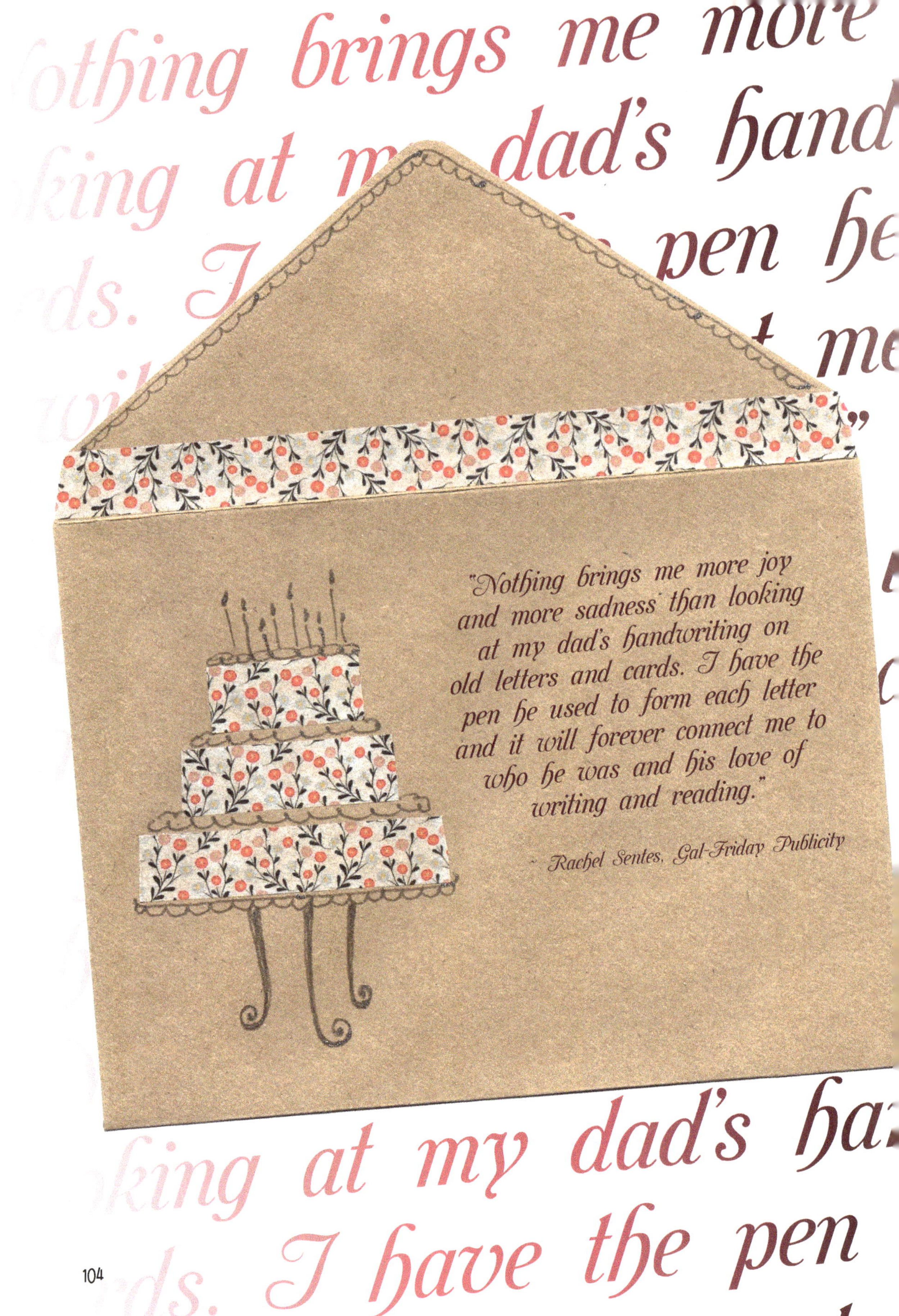
"Nothing brings me more joy
and more sadness than looking
at my dad's handwriting on
old letters and cards. I have the
pen he used to form each letter
and it will forever connect me to
who he was and his love of
writing and reading."
- Rachel Sentes, Gal-Friday Publicity

BUILD YOUR THEME AROUND AN EVENT

Traditional Holidays: Christmas, New Years, Valentine's Day, Easter, Halloween, Thanksgiving, or any major celebrations in your area or culture.

Life Events: birthday, graduation, engagement, wedding, anniversary, first/new baby, first/new pet, big move, first/new apartment, first/new house, first/new job, promotion, retirement, recent trips or vacations, etc.

Significant Anniversaries: classic literature (2018 is the 200th anniversary of Mary Shelley's Frankenstein), historic events (2019 is the 75th anniversary of D-Day), popular culture (2019 is the 80th anniversary of The Wizard of Oz), etc.

Annual Events: Dr. Seuss Day, Talk Like a Pirate Day, World Wildlife Day, Earth Day, World Bee Day, Mother's Day, Father's Day, etc.

Sporting Events: the Olympics, World Cup, Stanley Cup Finals, Tour de France, British Open, local tournaments, etc.

BUILD YOUR THEME AROUND FAVOURITE THINGS

These can be your favourites, certainly, but your choice will resonate more with your reader if you're both fans, or if you've selected something they love and adore.

Animals / Pets: think quirky critters like the sloth or the majestic narwhal, backyard creatures like squirrels and moles, oh-so-cute kittens or oh-so-huge giant breed dogs, animals associated with holidays, like ravens and Halloween, or wise owls, or elephants that never forget.

Movies: what movies have you seen recently and loved? Or is there one you and your reader went to together? Is your reader a Star Wars fan? A horror junkie? A classic film buff?

Music: folk, country, rock, blues, jazz, hip-hop, classical, Irish jigs on the fiddle, the Beatles, the Imagine Dragons, local talent, or the band you have/used to have in high school. There's much to build on here from individual instruments, sheet music and notes, album cover art, and song lyrics.

Foods: You can choose one item from or build around groupings like fruit, sweets, holiday foods, or favourite family recipes.

MAKE A LIST OF RELATED SYMBOLS OR IMAGES

Choose between three and five of the best symbols, with one being a standout that you'll use as your main visual element. A heart, a cupid, and an arrow for Valentine's Day - with the heart being the main visual. A cupcake, a present, and a candle for a birthday message - with the cupcake being the main visual. A torch, the Olympic rings, and your country's flag for the Olympics with the torch being the main visual, etc.

CREATE A COLOUR PALETTE, SPECIFIC PATTERN OR TEXTURE TO MATCH YOUR THEME

Holidays tend to highlight certain colours or colour patterns. Plaids for Christmas, fluffy, soft pastels for Spring, These colours, tones, and textures will help you choose just the right envelopes, paper, ink, markers, or paints. To keep things complimentary and visually appealing, don't go overboard with your selection. Again, choose the best 3 to 5 colours/patterns/textures so they work together as a team, rather than overwhelming or confusing your message.

MAKE A LIST OF POSSIBLE "CONFETTI" TO INCLUDE

It's fun to have little treats spilling out of the envelope when your reader opens it. These could be stickers or stamps you've found that relate to your theme, a ticket stub from a movie or concert, a hand-made bookmark, small cutouts of watercolour icons you've created, or a sketch you've done.

MAKE A LIST OF "TALKING POINTS" TO INCLUDE

This will be the bulk of your letter so do take some time to brainstorm ideas. What are your thoughts on the theme you've chosen? Why did you choose it? What does the theme remind you of? How does it related to your reader? Is there key information about the theme that you learned directly from the reader?

Do you have a theme-related story to share? Do you have words of encouragement for your reader? Does the theme you've chosen offer them support, or a fun way to congratulate them on a life event or recent success, or help cheer them on toward a distant goal?

Don't be disappointed if you do not receive a letter in response. Your message HAS made a difference, whether you receive formal acknowledgement, or not.

Gently prompting your reader for feedback or posing questions to them, may spark their own letter writing efforts.

And who knows, you may find your own mailbox graced with a bit of Happy Mail in return.

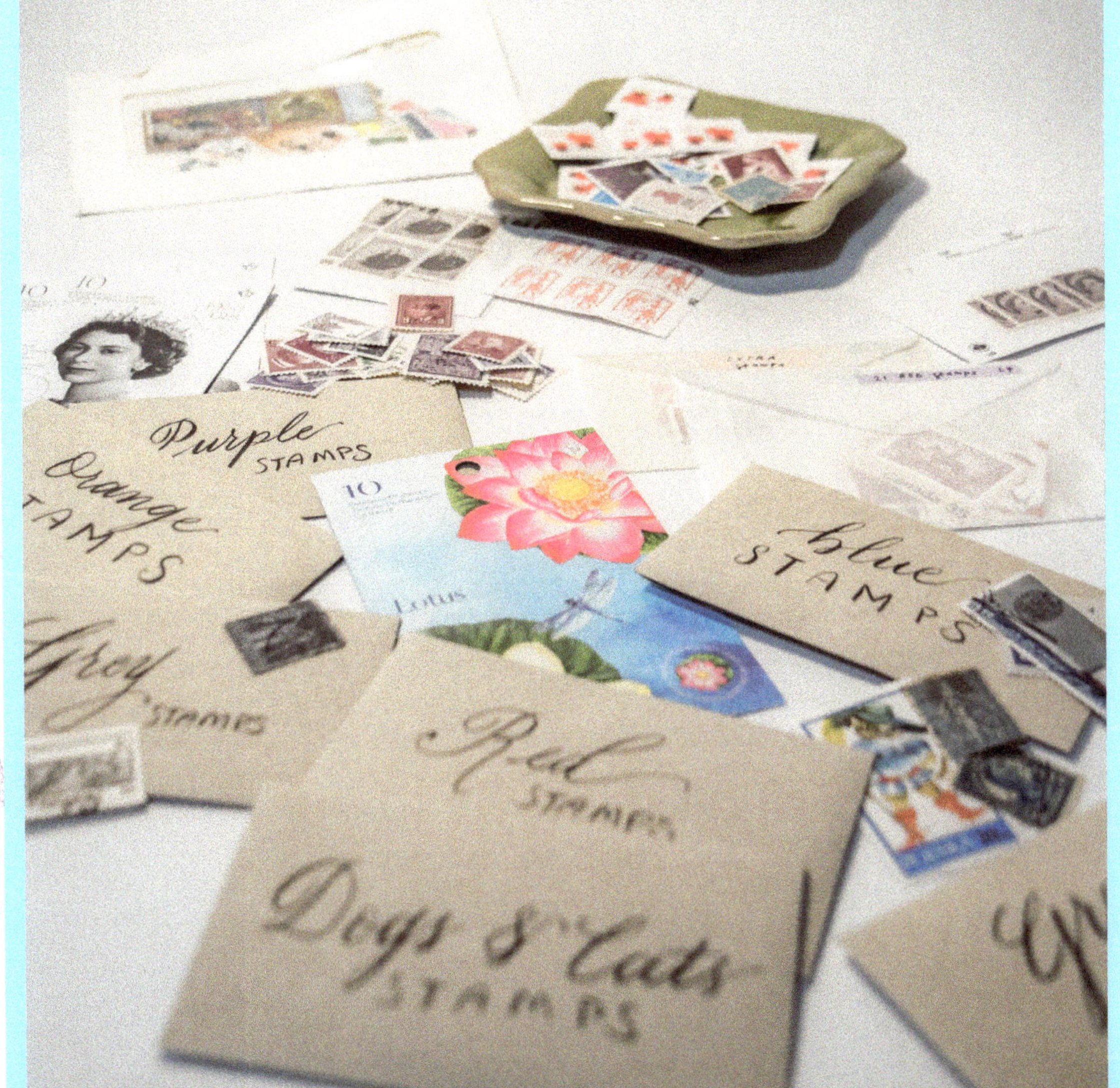

In this image: I love to decorate my Happy Mail envelopes with both current stamps and vintage ones which relate to my selected theme. I often pick up vintage stamps at garage sales and spend time dividing them up according to colour or theme for easy access at a later date.

MAKE A LIST OF QUESTIONS TO ASK

Questions are a good way to wrap up your letter by giving your reader a chance to mull on the theme and perhaps form a reply. Questions like: Has your reader done anything related to the theme lately? Do they have a theme-related story to share? What's their favourite pet, animal, movie, food, drink, etc? Are they excited for an upcoming event? How are they managing a challenging life event?

IN CONCLUSION

Always end with well wishes and a hope to hear from your reader soon. This is a final bit of positivity and encouragement that also leaves the door open for future correspondence.

The goal of Happy Mail is to reach out, hopefully connect with others, and to also spread positivity. It isn't a competition to see who can get the most replies. If you've found it a bit awkward to begin on your letter-writing journey, imagine that your reader would have the same feelings at first as well. YOU GOT THIS!

ENVELOP ART SAMPLES

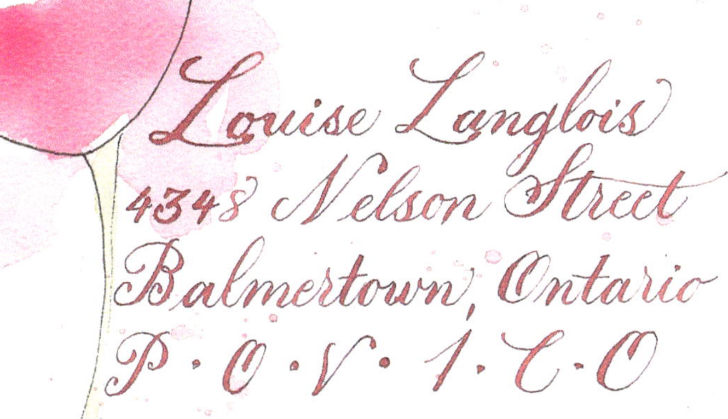

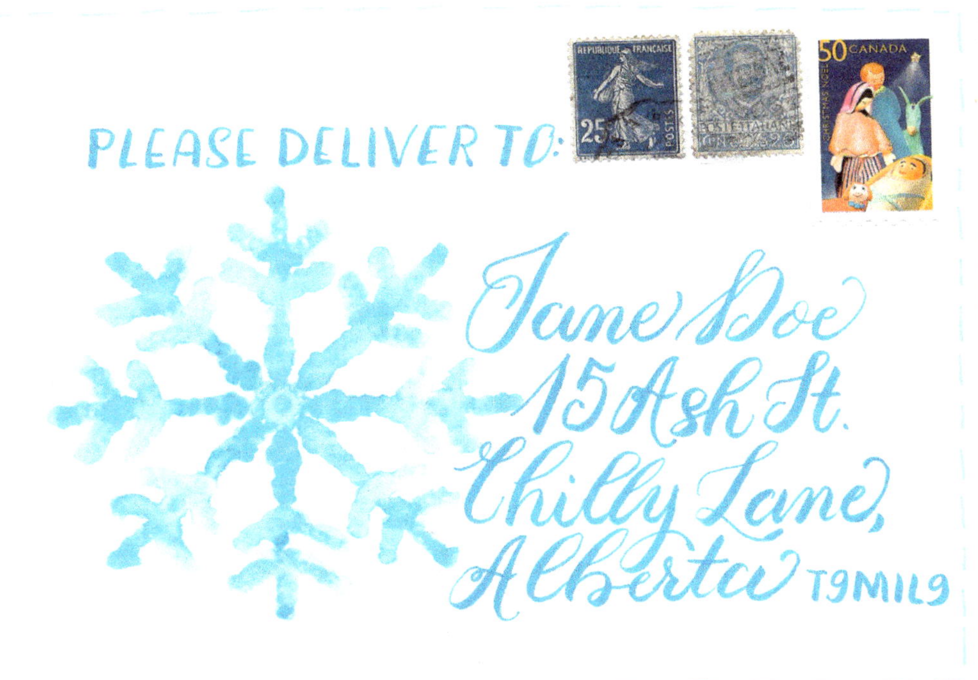

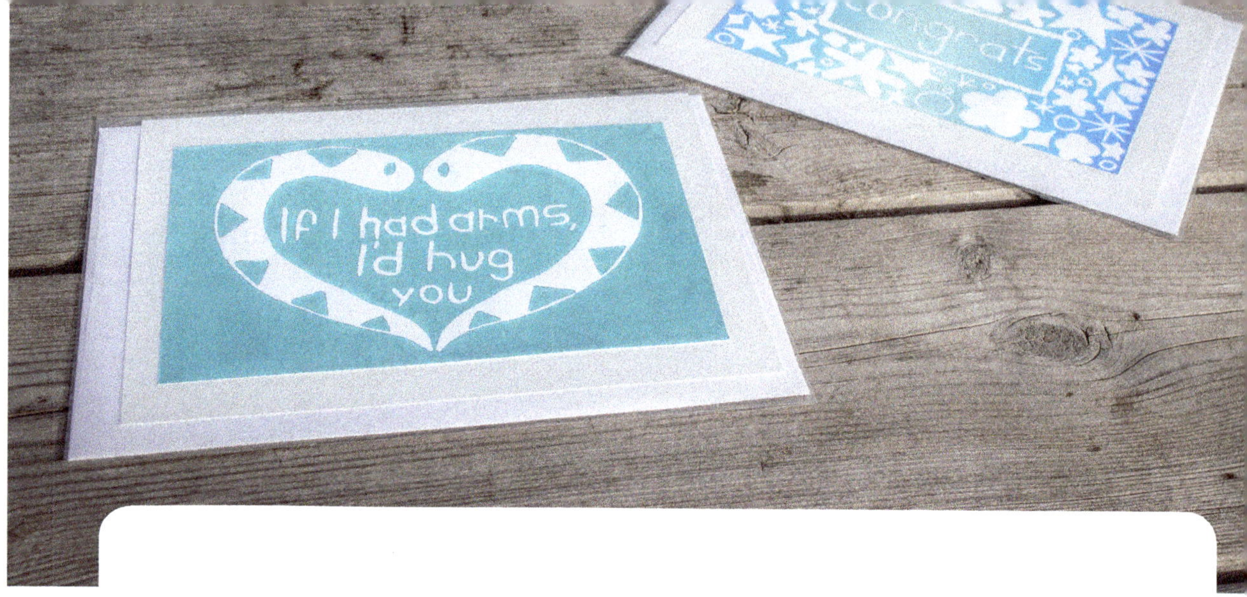

HAPPY MAIL IN ACTION

As I've mentioned, Happy Mail is a unique way to spread positivity and joy. It promotes mindfulness, contemplation and an intentional purpose to your lettering practice. From a more art-business side of things, it can also be an excellent way to promote your work AND support your community.

For example, meet Meghan Rennie from SunSoft Cards, a small greeting card designer based in my home town, Cold Lake, Alberta. Meghan is a bright young woman with many artistic talents. She writes fiction. She's a singer / songwriter. She illustrates, designs, and creates linocut greeting cards and although she's turned that particular skill set into a small business, she's found a way to promote herself while giving back at the same time.

Meghan kindly agreed to an interview for this book. Thanks again, Meghan! Below is our lake-side conversation in a nutshell. I think you'll find her perspective inspiring, I certainly do.

JG: How did you develop your linocutting skills?

MR: We learned the basics of linocutting in grade nine art class and I would stay after school and try new things. Eventually, through the school, I bought my own supplies to take home and took off after that.

JG: How did you get your small creative business up and running?

MR: Through our local "Biz Kid$" program. It's aimed at kids with an entrepreneurial spirit. With the drive and a business idea. Then they are partnered with a local businessperson as a mentor. They're also given seed money to fund their startup, but they have to take on all the responsibilities themselves. Coming up with a budget, doing reports. Every part of the program helps them build their business.

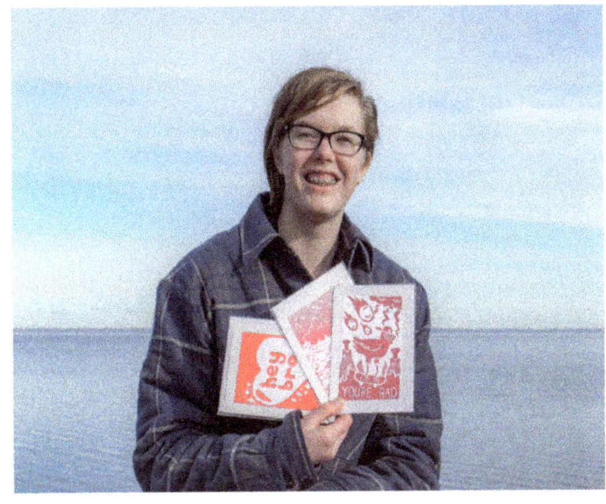

JG: Why greeting cards?

MR: There's a reason why the card market is still growing even though we have texting and email, and this and that and everything. It's because people love that personal connection.

JG: Have you received a card or letter that had an impact on you?

MR: My mom would write these lovely, heartfelt letters which I've always loved. I also attend YouthWrite, an Alberta-based writing camp for kids. They have this activity called "Mail" where you hand-write notes to the other campers. I have received some absolutely make-me-cry beautiful messages. It made me realize the power of letters and cards. Words are wonderful, but (when spoken) they're easy to forget sometimes. With a letter you can go back and re-read it when you need to.

JG: What does Happy Mail mean to you?

MR: I guess at it's core is a great intent to spread a legacy of love – that's one of those very dramatic sounding things but – we do a lot of self-promotion in our lives, so I think it's wonderful to give this bit of time and happiness to other people.

JG: How do you give back with your greeting card business?

MR: For every five cards I sell, I write a personal message in one and send it to the Ronald McDonald House in Edmonton. I prepare batches at a time and send them all at once as there are 32 families staying at the house. This way they all get one on the same day. I usually try to write something that's supportive for the parents, no matter what their situation might be, and for the kids, I include a little joke or a fun fact so there is something just for them. You may not think a card or hand-written message can change a life, but it's a start, and you will always have some sort of positive impact.

JG: What's the future look like for you and SunSoft Cards?

MR: I've been doing this for a year and a half now and I'm going to post secondary, so might have to take a bit of a hiatus, but I do want to continue. I love what I do. I'm hoping to take a combined degree in business and fine arts. I'm figuring it out as I go.

Follow Meghan on Instagram: @sunsoftart

ONE LAST THING: PAPER IS JUST THE BEGINNING

Once you have a handle on the letterforms, it's time to experiment with different brush pens and lettering surfaces. Below are a few projects I've completed as examples of what's possible, but surfaces to consider: pillow covers, wood signs, furniture, you can scan and incorporate your work into invitations, menus, or graphic designs, write on glass windows, mirrors, musical instruments, leather jackets, walls, leaves, rocks, beach glass, ceramic tiles, pottery, or create tattoo designs. Don't be afraid to try things out and get a bit messy. I know you'll do great things!

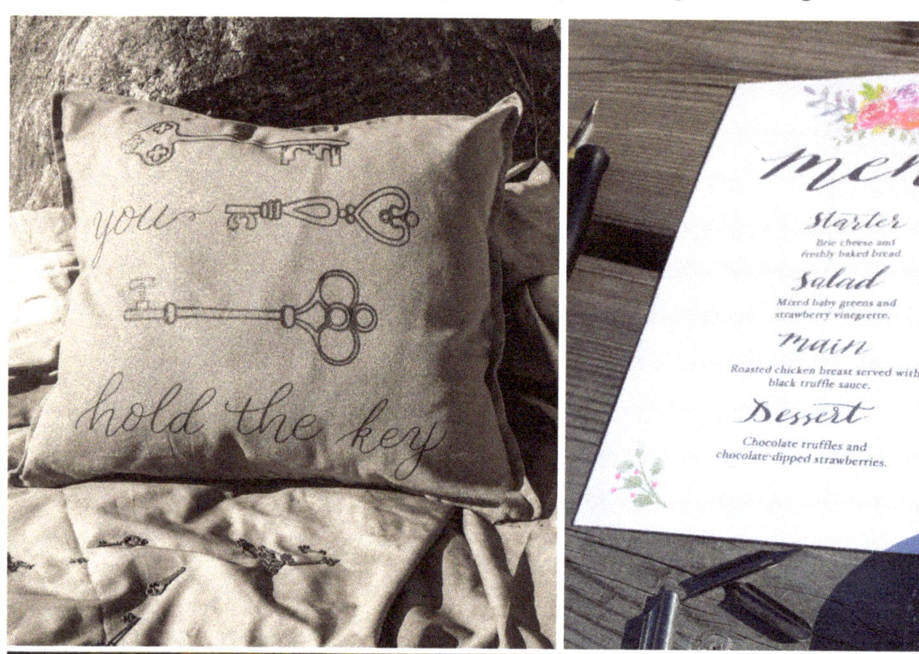

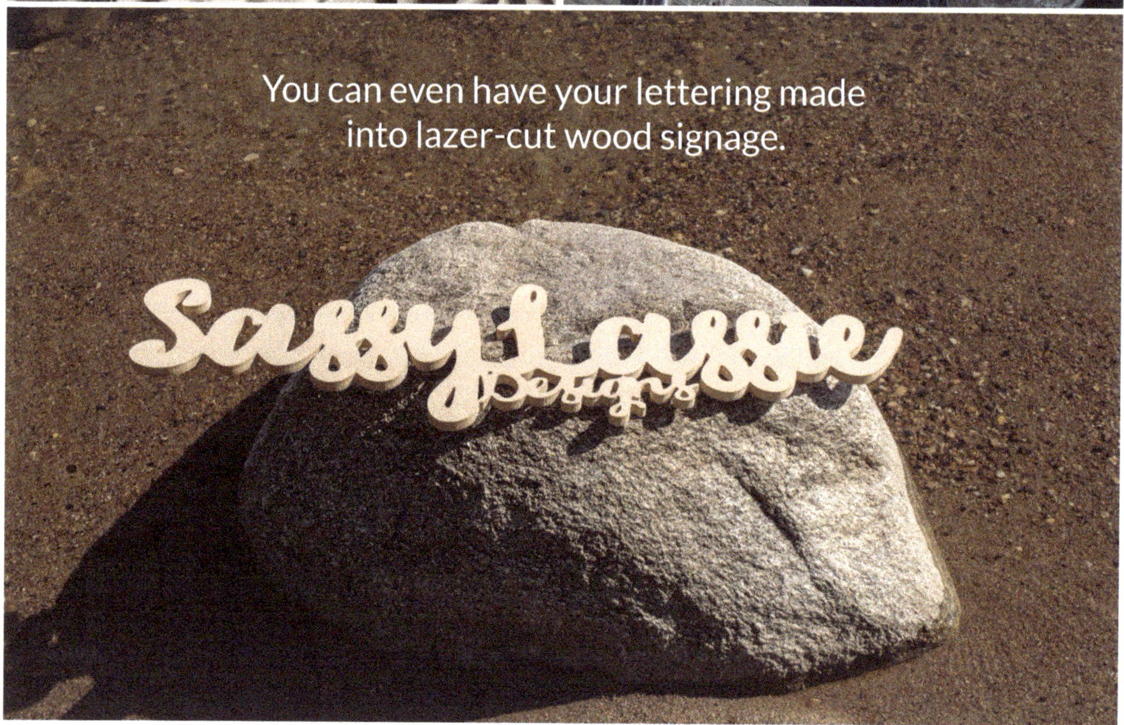

You can even have your lettering made into lazer-cut wood signage.

the templates

be you

you got this

Create

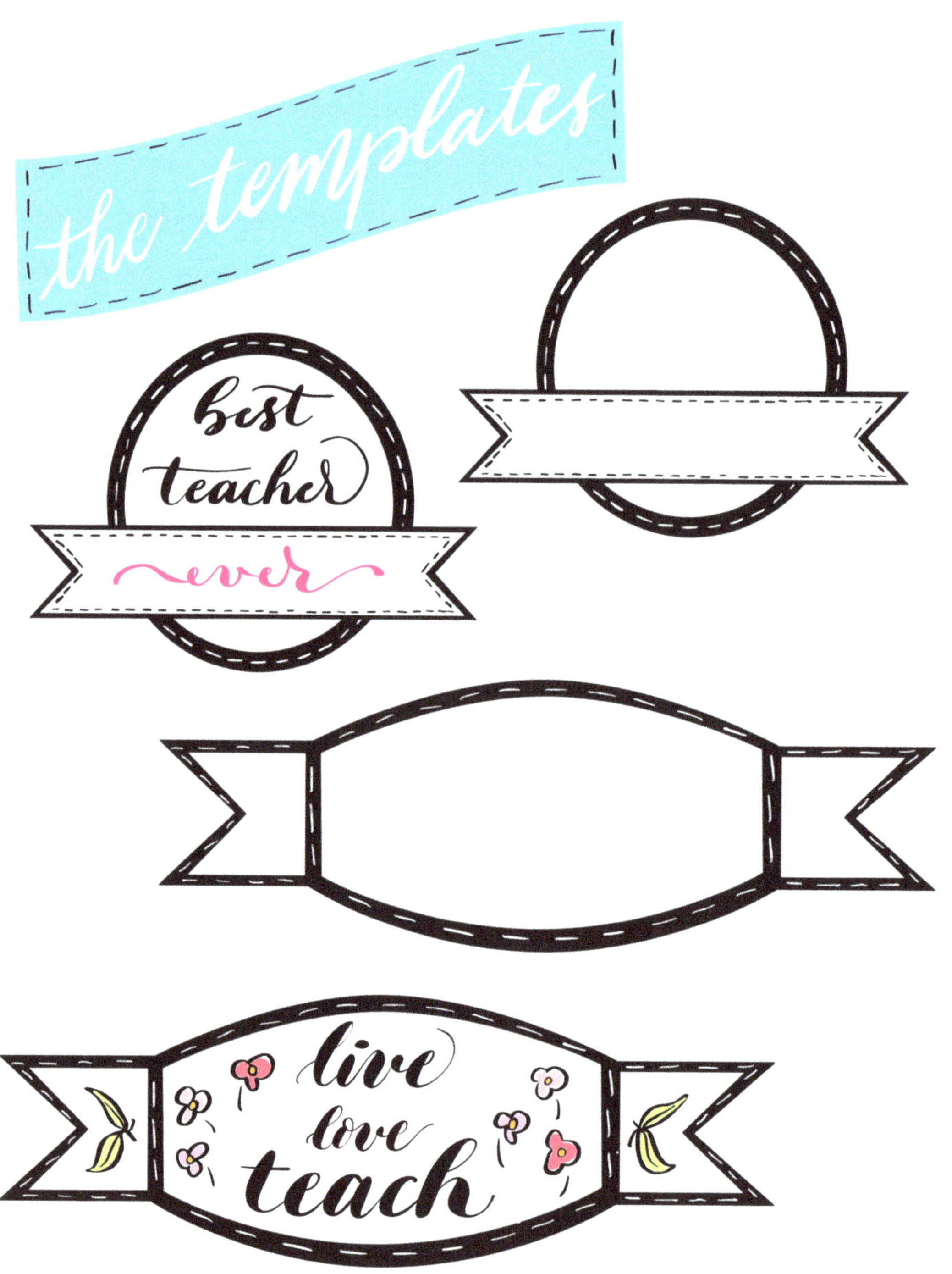
the templates
best teacher
ever
live love teach

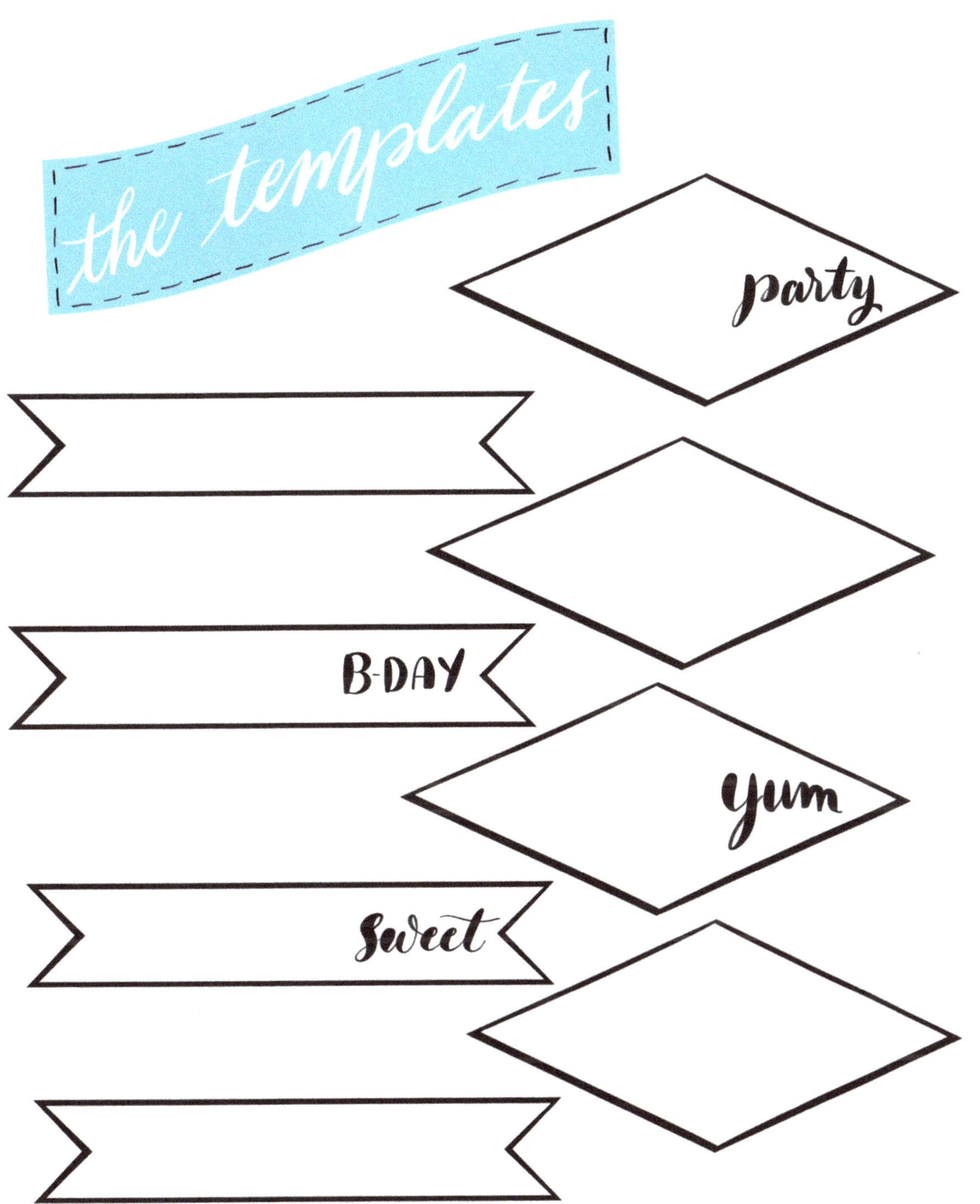
the templates
party
B-DAY
yum
Sweet

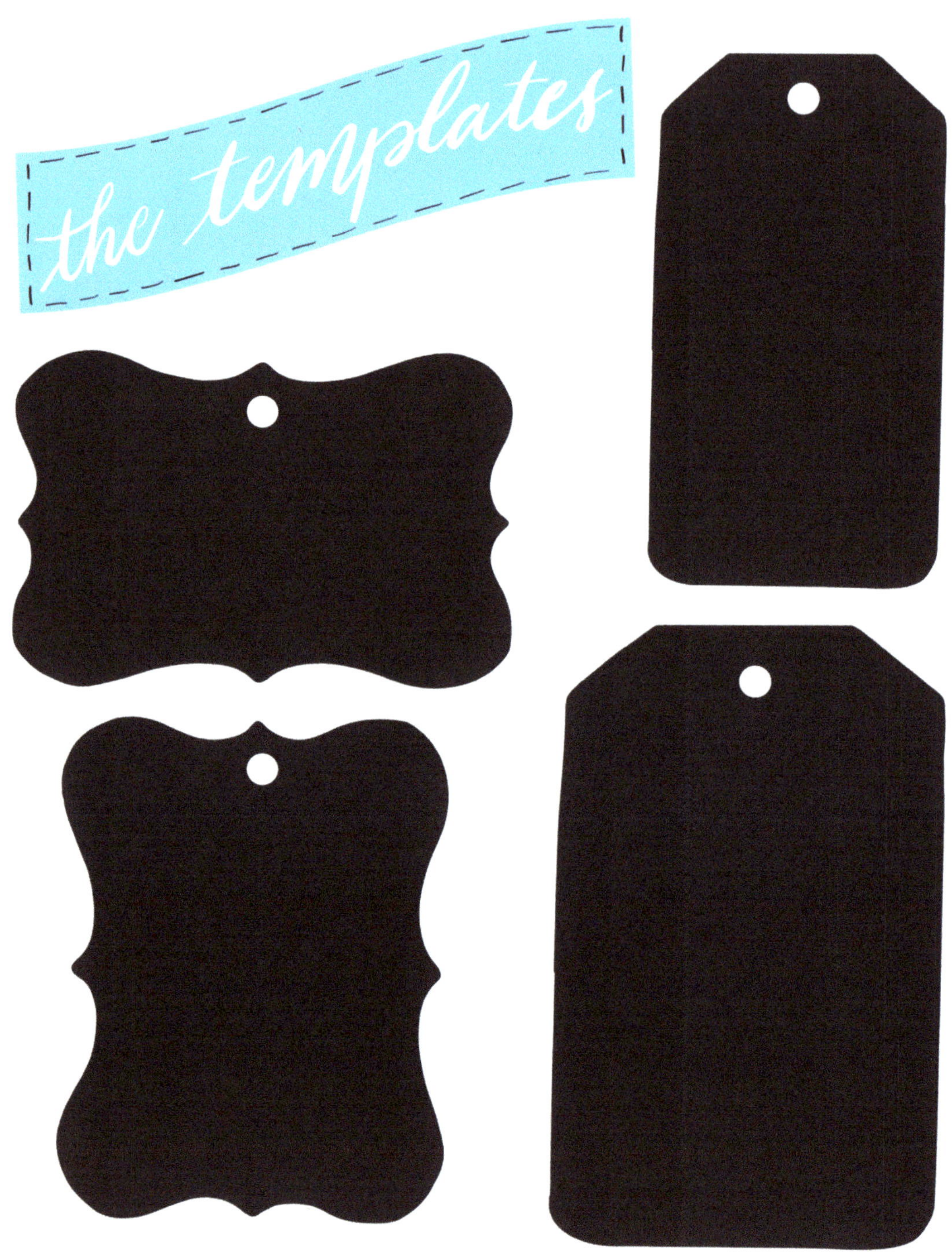
the templates

INDEX

ACKNOWLEDGEMENTS

I am, as always, thankful for my husband, who, after his initial, "You're doing what now?", fully supported my decision to step out of my fiction comfort zone and write this book. Thanks, my love.

Crazy Beautiful Letters wouldn't be anywhere near crazy beautiful without the talent and unfailing energy of Linda Goymer. Thanks so much for taking on this beast of a project with me. We did it. Whoopa!

To the beautiful mothers and daughters who joined me for a crazy day of crafting and lettering - YOU DID A FANTABULOUS JOB! - thanks ever so much for being excellent models.

I have consulted many lettering, calligraphy, and art resources over the last few years and thank the talented letterers and artists who graciously share their knowledge.

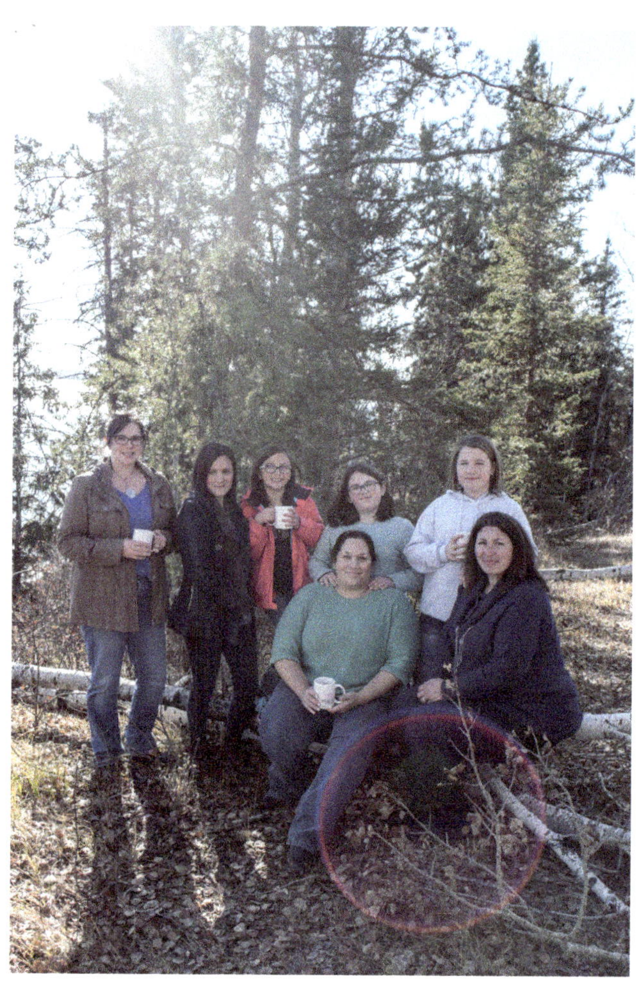

Learn. Create.
Share what you know.

That's what it's all about.

And finally, to you. Yes, YOU.
Thanks so much for reading.

Now go make some
crazy beautiful letters!

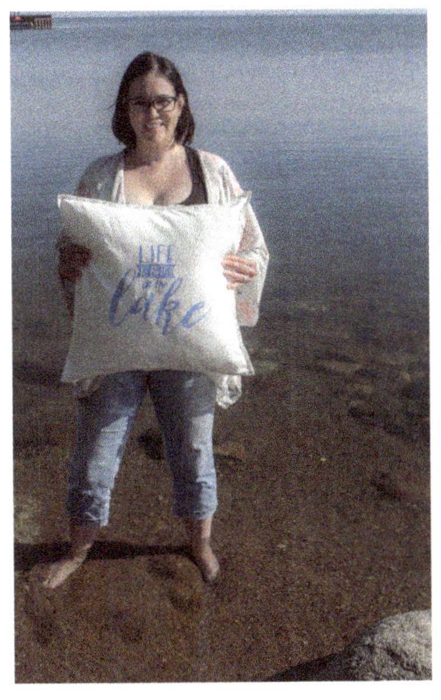

ABOUT THE AUTHOR

Judith Graves has multiple young adult novels and short stories published with Leap Books, Orca Book Publishers, Compass Press, and, under the pen name, Judith Tewes, is also published with Bloomsbury Spark. In addition, Judith is an award-winning screenwriter and playwright, an illustrator and hand-letterer who facilitates lettering and fiction writing workshops for both adults and young adults. She lives in northern Alberta with her husband and aDOGable fur kids.

Learn more about Judith at www.judithgraves.com

ABOUT THE PHOTOGRAPHER

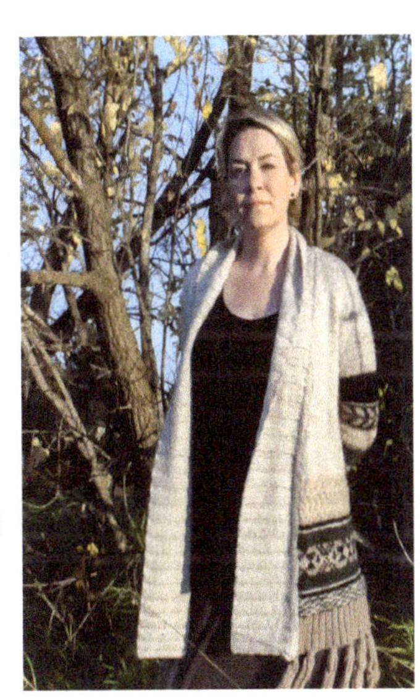

Linda Goymer, born and raised in Alberta, spends most of her time upcycling and being thrifty. She can most likely be found playing with her dog, the squirrels and enjoying nature. Linda's favourite passion is capturing and sharing beauty with her photography so it was an absolute pleasure to be chosen to take this journey with Judith. Linda is absolutely thrilled to be working with her and helping teach others how to create their own beauty.

Learn more about Linda at www.lindagoymer.com

Join the Crazy Beautiful Letters: Lettering with Sassy Lassie Facebook Group where you'll have access to further tips from Judith, as well as instructional videos.

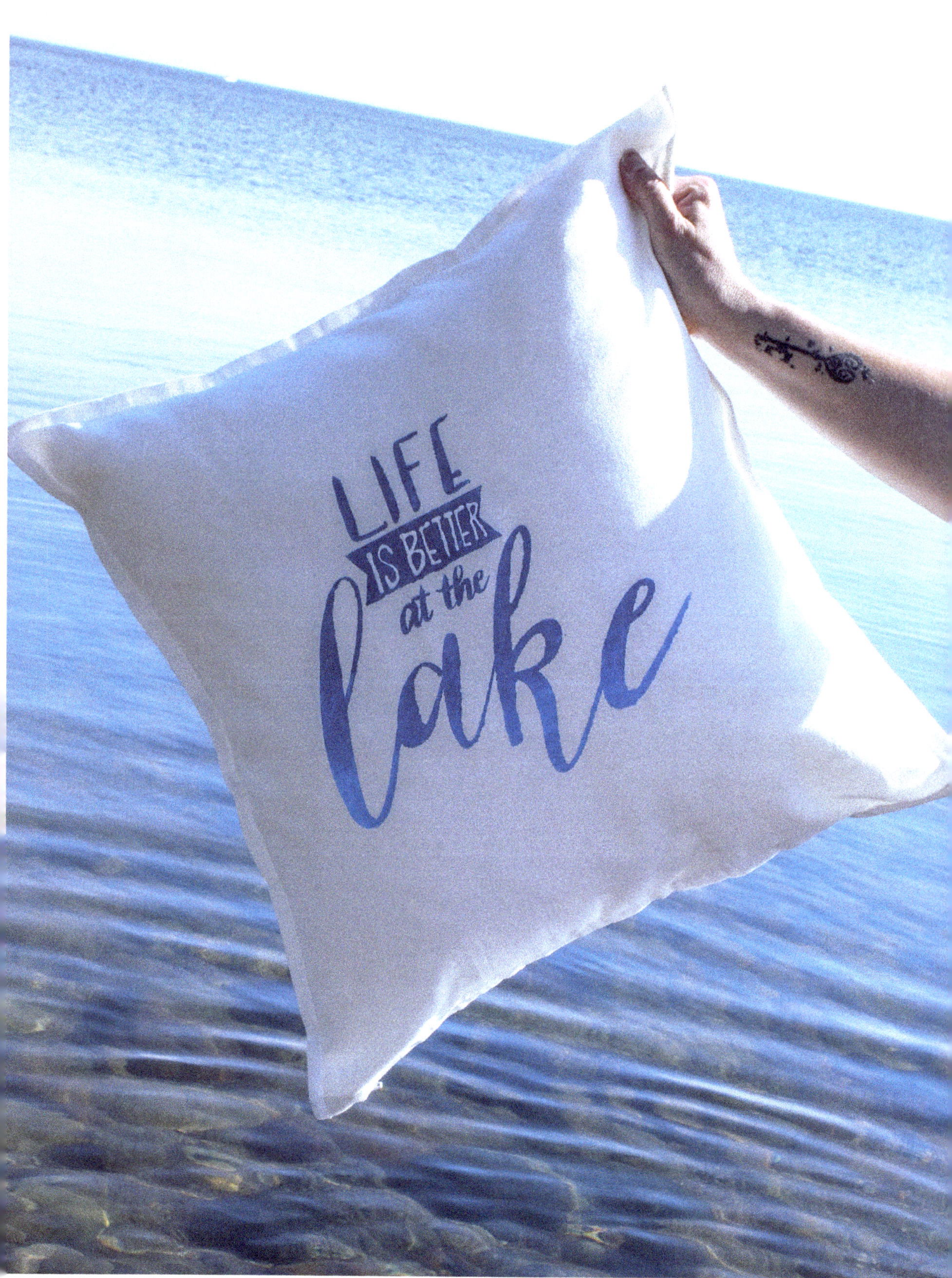
LIFE
IS BETTER
at the
lake

www.ingramcontent.com/pod-product-compliance
Ingram Content Group UK Ltd.
Pitfield, Milton Keynes, MK11 3LW, UK
UKHW061954290726
14090UKWH00021B/1227